M000076948

THE PROBLEM ISN'T THEIR PAYCHECK

THE
PROBLEM
ISN'T THEIR
PAYCHECK

How to Attract Top Talent and
Build a Thriving Company Culture

GRANT BOTMA

LIONCREST
PUBLISHING

COPYRIGHT © 2019 GRANT BOTMA

All rights reserved.

THE PROBLEM ISN'T THEIR PAYCHECK

How to Attract Top Talent and Build a Thriving Company Culture

ISBN   978-1-5445-0543-5 *Hardcover*

       978-1-5445-0541-1 *Paperback*

       978-1-5445-0542-8 *Ebook*

       978-1-5445-0544-2 *Audiobook*

This book is dedicated to my team, who are unbelievably hardworking and love people well. You are family.

CONTENTS

INTRODUCTION

In the United States, 87.7 percent of employees are not working up to their full potential.[1]

When you read that statistic, how do you feel?

Do you wonder if it's true? Are you curious how that number can be so high? That stat is almost unbelievable—but it's completely true. To get to that number, Deloitte surveyed three thousand US workers who worked at least thirty hours per week across fifteen different industries, at all different job levels from frontline sales to middle management to senior positions. This study was extremely comprehensive, so we can trust its accuracy.

Or do you not have to wonder if that number is correct?

---

1   https://www2.deloitte.com/insights/us/en/topics/talent/worker-passion-employee-behavior.html

Do you already know that it's true? You can feel it; you know that most employees do not live up to their potential, because you see it every day.

Maybe your first reaction was, "Yeah, I know. My team isn't living up to their potential, and as a result, *I have to pick up the slack.*"

Maybe by this point, you're numb. You don't feel anything when you read that statistic because you're too tired to care.

Whatever you feel—or don't feel—right now, the numbers don't lie. There are a shockingly high number of people going to work every day and not fulfilling their potential.

But who cares, right? How does that affect you?

FROM A BURDENSOME BUSINESS...

When you have a team of people who are not living up to their potential, the joy you once had in owning a business dies.

You give your employees a job, you help provide for them and their families by giving them an income, and you're left wondering, *Shouldn't they do better? Can't they do more?* You're frustrated that they're not giving their best. And then, after investing so much time and energy into teaching those employees how to do their jobs, you get to the point where you depend on them—and they just leave.

Out of nowhere, seemingly on a whim, your employees can just say, "See you later," whenever they want.

That hurts. It erodes your trust in people. After such a terrible experience hiring people who ultimately don't work out, who can blame you for saying, "I'm never doing *that* again!" You got burned.

And where does that leave you? You become an owner-operator instead of the owner. The entire business and all the daily operations depend on you. You literally cannot take a vacation. You have the money to do so, but if you even try, you can't go anywhere without being tied to your phone the entire trip.

You're profitable because you have a great business. You have a product or service that people need. You likely don't have a problem getting customers to pay you, but you have no idea how to scale your business. Externally, you appear successful. You're making money and you have ambitions—you know you should be doing more—but you can't because you don't have time. Every second is spent maintaining your current customer base and executing on existing business—instead of looking for ways to level up.

This isn't what you wanted when you started your own business—and this isn't how you want to continue. Maybe you've even thought about selling the business just to get your life back. You've worked so hard...for what?

You're tired of the hustle. Your family is tired, too. Your kids miss you, and your spouse wants you back. The business has gone from something you pursued together to a point of contention in all the relationships that matter most to you.

You want to enjoy it again. You want to have your business be the provision that you always dreamed it would be. You want a lot of income, yes, but you want freedom, too. Free time—more time with your family—but also freedom to act on the ideas and creativity and entrepreneurial spirit that you have within you.

You want to get out of the daily operations. You want to stop selling. And you want to do the things you care about. You want to have a trusted team of people who support you and your business so you can grow and impact more people. With this in place, you will be acting on the most valuable ideas you have inside you.

You see that other businesses are doing this. If they can do it, why can't you?

...TO JOYFUL JOBS

Let me be very clear: you absolutely *can* do this, and I'm going to show you how.

I'll show you not only how to attract amazing people to build the team you want, but I'll also reveal a motivational hierarchy that exists within all of us—allowing you to retain these awesome people and get the most out of them. With this new framework for motivating your employees, you can experience the freedom of a business that is truly thriving. You can spend time doing the things that matter most *to you*.

Your company can go to levels you never thought of before. You can achieve a level of growth you never expected, receive awards and accolades you didn't even know existed—all of which points to making more of an impact on your community than you ever imagined when you first started your business.

Instead of being told that you're successful, you can actually *feel it*. You have an overall sense of amazing gratitude for your team, your life, and everything that's brought you as far as you've come. You have a level of pride that you've never had before. You're proud of your success, and you are so proud of your team, but more importantly, you're proud of the huge impact you're making on people.

You will feel deeper joy and pride because there's so much substance behind it.

And where does all this substance come from? Something as simple and straightforward as making a mindset shift in the way you motivate your employees. Creating a company culture where each and every person makes a difference. Building a business where people—including you!—can flourish.

After making this paradigm shift, there's no way you would ever consider selling your business. Even when you retire, you may not get out of your business completely. Retirement, for you, might mean continuing to scale your team and your growth so that your role transitions into being an ambassador for the business. A person who comes into the office to give high fives and write checks. A leader on fire with the amazing impact being made on other people.

You'll find so much joy and meaning in doing what you were meant to do that it's what you want to do forever. You can even create a place that the people you love the most—your children—can be a part of. Your business can go from being the burden it currently is to ultimately becoming your legacy.

How do I know all of this to be true? Because I'm living it!

LEARNING ON THE JOB

Like most people who start their own businesses, nobody taught me how to be a CEO. I had to figure that out all on my own. You've likely been in the same position—trying to be the owner, operator, lead salesperson, janitor, even the IT person. Every area of your business is dependent on you, each and every day.

My business was doing well enough; we provided a great service with a really great product and people were coming to us, so we didn't have a problem getting business. But I didn't know how to manage my tiny team—or how to attract more talent. I read conventional management books and tried to implement the techniques they offered. I looked back at what I had learned in college, earning a degree in business. I tried to recall all the traditional pieces of wisdom associated with being the boss.

And then one of my employees quit—at the time, that was a large percentage of my workforce!—and that hurt. I was forced to pick up the slack, and that required making major changes to my business. I started sleeping on a couch in my office.

I didn't go home for days in a row, just trying to serve as many customers as I could. They were coming in the door like crazy, which was awesome, but I felt terrible that I wasn't at home with my wife and our new babies. I had set out to provide an awesome service for my community while also providing for my family, but I just didn't have enough bandwidth. There wasn't enough of me.

After weeks of this, I said to myself, "I can't do it anymore. *There's got to be a different way of running this business.*"

Fortunately, my family had a get-together around that time—one of the few I didn't miss because I was too busy working. My uncle listened to how I was doing and asked, "Grant, why did you start the business?"

"To make an impact on people," I replied.

"Okay," he said, "but you can make only so much impact on your own. You need to replicate yourself. The more people you have working as extensions of you, the greater the impact you can have."

"I get that, but I don't trust anybody to do it the way I do it."

He said, "No one will do it the exact way you do—and that's okay. They just need to do it close enough to the way you do it. And you need to learn to trust people."

That conversation challenged me. I had to take a look in the mirror and evaluate my actions—and my motives. I realized that the management books and the traditional way of leading people was wrong. It didn't align with my goals, and it was hurting my company culture.

After that realization, I threw out all those management books. Instead of studying how to supervise people, I studied how people thought, why we do the things we do, and how we're motivated. I dedicated myself to better understanding how the human brain is wired, soaking up every book, magazine article, YouTube video, podcast, and scientific study about social science. In my own right, I became a behavioral scientist.

Armed with this knowledge and the desire to make a bigger impact than ever before, I did one of the hardest things I have ever done in my life: I hired four more people and decided I was done being customer-facing. I wasn't going to do the mortgages, insurance, or investments anymore—I was going to run the company.

That journey was incredibly difficult, but it turned out to be one of the best things I've ever done. Sure, it allowed me to spend more time away from the office to be with my family, but it also allowed me to grow the company in ways I had previously only dreamed of. Now, when I am in the office, I'm working on the things I *want* to do rather than stuff I *have* to do. I'm doing things that allow us to scale, the things that are most valuable—to my team, my business, and our community.

Now, when I go on vacations, I leave my phone at the hotel. I don't make phone calls. I'm not saying they don't happen—they do; it's part of business—but I have a team of people handling those calls at the right moment. And the beautiful thing is that they now handle those calls better than I ever could. Their expertise, under my leadership, has created a team of people who are masters of their craft.

A PARADIGM SHIFT

This book gives you a new way to think about your business and how you work.

I used to be chained to my business. Now I leave whenever I want. Just before writing this book, I took my family on an extended vacation in Hawaii. While I was away, my team broke records. They thrive when I'm out of town. Instead of me trying to tackle every opportunity that comes our way, I trust my team to handle it—even better than I could.

It's fun to turn a profit and it's important to provide for your family, but that's just money. As you're going to learn in upcoming chapters, money motivation isn't sustainable—for you or your team.

The framework I lay out creates a paradigm shift in how you manage your team. It will help you attract the people you need so you can build a thriving team who can take your business to new heights.

How do I know? When I started my business, it was just a small mortgage company. Now we're a mortgage, insurance, and investment management company that was recently awarded with *Inc.*'s 5,000 fastest-growing companies in the entire nation.

With this framework in place, you'll learn to:

- Stop thinking of money as the primary motivator for your team
- Create freedom for your employees so that they develop an ownership mentality
- Use affirmation to build your team's confidence
- Create a unified purpose that gives your business a north star—something that everyone pursues together, so you can make a bigger impact on the community you serve

WARNING: If you're reading this book to try and pay your employees as little as humanly possible, stop reading and go get a refund on the book. This book is not about trying to take advantage of people in our community and our society.

It's about intentionally creating a workplace that gives employees more than money. It's about creating a culture that attracts top talent—and then helps that talent thrive. This book is about turning around the stat I shared to open this book.

The fact that 88 percent of employees are not working to their potential is wrong. Employees have more in them, they desire more, so they deserve more. They deserve to work to their full potential. And you, as an employer, deserve to have their very best so that, together, your business can make the biggest impact possible.

FOR LEADERS AND JOB SEEKERS

But what if you're not a business owner or manager? In fact, what if you're not an employer at all? What if you are someone looking for a good job? How can you evaluate prospective employers to see if theirs is a company where you'd like to work?

The motivational hierarchy is true of all individuals.

You're looking for freedom. You want to be affirmed that you are in the right place, doing the right thing. You're looking to do work that matters. You don't want to leave a job every three to four years, but statistics tell us that's what is happening. You don't like that fact, but at the same time, you don't like working for an employer who doesn't give you a purpose. You don't like working for a place that doesn't give you freedom and affirmation.

You may know that you want these motivators, but maybe you're not sure how to articulate them. Even more importantly, you might not know how to identify a business that truly acts on them. But I want you to know that there *are* businesses out there that do a great job motivating employees using freedom, affirmation, and purpose.

Reading this book can help give you the mindset you will need to properly assess a potential employer—whether you are coming out of college or you're one of the statistically proven 51 percent of currently employed people who are looking for a new place to work. You want to find the best company that fits with what you need. You want to find an awesome job, one that you'll appreciate and be able to thrive in—and one you'll be able to stay in so you don't feel like you need to look for a new job every few years, only to be disappointed again.

You want to work for a company where the work you do

makes the world a better place. Somewhere you're appreciated, in a job that gives you freedom. This book will help you identify those companies.

And if you're not a job seeker—if you are the manager or business owner this book is primarily written for—this section is to give you awareness that you can hand this book to someone who *is* looking for a great place to work. Part of being a great leader is giving people the tools they need to find what they're looking for—and you're in the perfect position to offer that guidance.

REBUTTAL

Even as you work through this paradigm shift and learn how to implement some of these new ideas, you might come up against some resistance, either internally with yourself or externally with other people. To address that resistance, you'll see a section called "Rebuttal" at the end of every chapter.

You know that you have an amazing product or service, but you may be standing in your own way when it comes to taking your business to the next level. You have to get out of your way, start trusting other people, and learn how to manage a team differently.

You may have a hard time applying the ideas in this book

because of your pride. It's difficult to hear that you may need to learn how to manage a team differently, to start trusting other people. Everyone around you is already telling you that you're successful. Your bank account is doing fine. But you're going to have a moment of realization: "This isn't good enough. I deserve better than this, my business can be more than this, and I want to make a bigger impact."

You probably have some rebuttals to what I'm saying right about now.

"But, Grant," you may be thinking, "I don't have time to read another book. It will take time—hours that I could be working, sleeping, or spending with my family."

That's why this book is relatively short, totally straightforward, and contains absolutely no fluff. I'm not going to waste your time. I'm going to include only what is genuinely helpful and gives you the answers you need. I respect the time and energy you're putting into this transformation.

In fact, you don't even have to read this book. You can find it on Audible, and a professional narrator with a silky-smooth voice will read it to you! If you do what I do and increase the reading pace to 1.5 or 2 times the speed, you'll go through the pages faster and will potentially retain more because you have to focus more. To level up your experience even more, try reading along as you listen. This combination of visual and auditory learning will increase retention exponentially.

This is not a sacred text; it's an opportunity to learn and grow. If you want to hold the pages and flip through it, try using a highlighter as a bookmark. Highlight things you'd like to try so that when you've finished reading, you can quickly flip back and see where to take action. When something resonates with you, underline it, write your own ideas, and take notes. Don't treat this book as delicate and precious. Dog-ear the pages. Mark it up!

This is your study guide, your resource for how to move forward in your business. At the end of each chapter, you're going to see two sections to help with your learning: the first calls out three main takeaways from that chapter, to drive home the key points, and the second is a place to write down your immediate thoughts and action steps. This allows you to get what's in your head down on paper so you have it to refer back to later as you begin to implement these strategies.

But don't put undue pressure on yourself to finish this book within a certain time frame. There's no deadline. If you commit to reading just one section—not even a full chapter—every day, it will take you only five or ten minutes a day and you'll still get through it pretty quickly.

You might have the best intentions of finishing this book, but the only thing that's going to help you get through it is being intentional about your actions. You are going to see a repeated theme, one that I also use when I speak and as I lead my team: "The best intentions require intentional actions." Taking action requires having a plan, so put it in your calendar. Try to schedule out how many sections you want to read each day.

Or you may be thinking, "I just don't know if I can do it."

I can tell you that you can do this. These steps are not complicated; they are intentionally simple, doable, and effective. The results are going to give you the freedom and ability to scale and thrive.

And you are not alone. It may feel like what you're going through is unique to your situation, but statistics tell us otherwise: if nearly 88 percent of employees aren't working up to their full potential, a lot of other small business owners are experiencing the same thing you are. You don't need to be ashamed of this.

You're in the right place—you're going to learn how to change your company culture and build a thriving team.

I was a kid who grew up on a farm, kicking cow patties for fun. There's nothing overly intelligent about me. I'm not going to speak over your head. The information I share is going to be relatable and practical, simple and easy to implement.

By the time you're finished reading this book, you will have a very simple framework that will completely change the way you engage with your team. It'll change your business. And it'll change your life.

FLIP THE SWITCH

Allow me to remind you that 88 percent of employees are not working to their full potential. That number is big and scary. Eighty-eight percent of the workforce is significant. Essentially, nine out of every ten people who work are underperforming.

But let's look at the flipside: it's not 100 percent, and that can give you hope. There's still that remaining 12.3 percent of employees who are working at or exceeding their potential. We can focus on those people, study how they work and what motivates them, to determine what makes them exceptional.

In that survey, the employees who fell into that 12.3 percent had something important in common: they had a purpose. There is meaning in what they do, in showing up to the office and in the tasks they complete every day. They are trying to make the world a better place, and they feel like what they are doing makes a big impact on people.

With this framework in place, your team can become part of that 12.3 percent. Your business can scale to levels of growth that were impossible before. And you don't have to have a large team to do it.

When people see the number of customers we serve at Stewardship, they assume I have at least three times the number of employees I actually have on my team. Because those employees are in the 12.3 percent, they are able to accomplish in two or three months what it takes most people a year to do. My team blows the national average out of the water. And they're not working eighty hours a week. They're not chained to their desks. They go home, spend time with their families—even have time to volunteer for the causes that mean the most to them.

But those national averages for production are lower than they otherwise could be—in fact, lower than they *should* be—because 87.7 percent of people don't work up to their potential.

My entire team is made up of only people in that 12 percent. We don't have any of the other 88 percent. Get ready to learn what you need to do to create a team of employees who are all in that 12 percent. As you'll see in the next chapter, it starts with you.

KEY TAKEAWAYS

- If you're like most people, reading this introduction is creating emotion. Hopefully, you're motivated. Inspired. Or, at the very least, excited. I want you to take that excitement and see it through to the end. I want you to not only finish this book, but to also implement changes that will make an impact on your business and on your life.

- One of the best ways for you to see an endeavor through to the end is by making a public profession that you are engaged in it. I want to invite you to share with people that you're reading this book. Take a picture or screenshot and send it to somebody. Or even better, post it on social media. Share your excitement with others!

- Tag me in the post (@grantbotma on Instagram and Twitter; Culture Course on Facebook at https://www.facebook.com/Culture-Course-277174859791250/) and I'll do my best to publicly engage with you and encourage you to keep going!

MY INTENTIONAL ACTIONS

....

....

....

....

....

....

....

....

....

....

....

....

CHAPTER 1

MINDSET SHIFT

Since first starting Stewardship in 2007, only a handful of employees have ever left the company.

Mike was the first employee who left—but it was entirely my fault. He has a heart of gold and is one of the most trustworthy people on the face of the planet. I told you a little about him in the introduction. I managed him the way the classic management books told me to. You know the ones I'm talking about—the techniques that say we're supposed to create goals that are just out of our employees' reach. They work their hardest to achieve those goals, always getting close but never quite hitting the moving target despite most likely accomplishing more than they otherwise would have. The advice in these management books believes that in order to get the most out of employees, you have to *squeeze* it out of them.

I followed these tactics to the letter, which led to killing Mike's confidence. There was no affirmation and zero real purpose behind those goals. I failed miserably as a leader and as a manager.

Unsurprisingly, that did not work well for him. Not only did he not produce well, but he was also unbelievably discouraged—almost on the verge of tears at one point. I actually did shed tears because I was making this human being's life worse.

Mike came to me and told me he couldn't do it anymore. He hated his job, and he wanted to go find something he could be good at.

So he returned to his former job at a local university—the job he'd held before coming to work for me. As far as affirmation is concerned, this was a better job for Mike. He felt like he was way better at that than he was at mortgages.

But the one thing I had done right when he worked for me is I gave him freedom. There was no clocking in or out. I didn't completely understand the importance of autonomy to the level we have now, but he had a lot of freedom to come and go.

At this new job, he felt like he was working for "the man," clocking in, clocking out, with no meaning or importance to the work he was doing. Mike went to work because he had to.

Because he appreciated the freedom I had given him, Mike came to me and asked for his job back. I said all right, of course—he's a hard worker and an amazing person. But I recognized that we'd had an issue before and decided that I was not going to ruin the affirmation piece this time.

We stopped having the traditional employee performance reviews with those impossible stretch goals. Instead, I did a new thing called an employ*er* review, where he reviewed me. Rather than destroying his confidence with goals I knew he wasn't going to hit, I asked questions to express my genuine care for him. I learned about his needs as an employee and acted on them as his leader.

As a result, Mike started doing better. He had more confidence, he produced really well, and he was thriving.

But because I didn't connect everything Mike was doing with a purpose, he still felt as if his job didn't have meaning. That's two jobs in a row where he was just working because he had to, not doing work that made the world a better place. Mike is a dream employee. He's extremely intelligent, very trustworthy, and a high performer. But because I didn't have a great purpose in my business, and

I couldn't put the things he did to that purpose, he was open to other opportunities.

So what did he do? He and his wife went to Thailand as missionaries fighting the sex trafficking trade. I mean, just the description of that job makes it clear he was making the world a better place.

Viewed objectively, the new job could be considered worse in almost every way. It paid much less and required Mike and his family to move to a different country. At the time he left, Mike was doing very well, producing at high levels and making a good living for his family. Yet he left to find *purpose*.

When Mike left that second time, I ended up sleeping at the office and trying to do all the work myself. By then, I had come to depend on his amazingly high level of production. He had done well handling an important sub-section of my business. His exit meant that I had to pick up the slack, and my business started to feel like a burden instead of a blessing. That's when I knew I had to change.

Part of that change involved evaluating why such a talented employee would want to leave. Why did he seek a job that paid significantly less, involved much more difficult work, and required uprooting and transplanting his entire family? Why didn't he see the same purpose in my business that I did? Because it was still in my head. I hadn't formally created a purpose, defined it, and woven it into my business.

So I sat down and figured out our unified purpose, using the same process I'll teach you to create yours. I used it to hire amazing new talent and create a growing, thriving company culture. And then I unified our entire team around that purpose.

When Mike came back from Thailand four years later, I had completely changed how we do things at Stewardship. Our internal culture was so different and so much better. We had a clear purpose, the entire team was on board with that purpose, and Stewardship had become one of the most attractive places to work in my community.

I had a list of more than one hundred qualified people who expressed a desire to be a part of my team—and Mike was one of them. I happily asked him to come back to work for me, and now he runs one of the most profitable divisions of my company. He does work that matters, his life has more meaning through his employment, and he feels the impact that he makes on the community.

IT'S TIME TO MAKE A SHIFT

If every small business owner were to list the worst qualities of the worst employees they've ever had, I guarantee that all of them would have selfishness in common.

Managers who use money to motivate their teams contribute to creating a selfish culture, one in which employees don't perform well. They look at the clock instead of seeing how they can better serve customers. They use the business simply as a means to get a paycheck, rather than becoming part of a team that works hard to make an impact on people.

Business owners with a money-motivating mindset don't have self-directed employees who consistently take initiative and do whatever is necessary to innovate and create an awesome experience for customers; they have people who show up and do the least amount of work possible to keep getting paid.

In the long run, these business owners have a team of people who are not going to be there. Employees are going to leave this company and move on to the next that offers more money. Can you blame them? They took the job because of money, showing that they're incentivized by money. If another opportunity comes up where they can get even more money, they're going to take it!

This puts the owner in the position of trying to have the highest comp plan possible, and at some point, that's just not going to work. They won't be able to pay people any higher. There's a limit to what small business owners are able to pay; their financials may not be the same as their competition. It's been proven over and over again that money motivation is not sustainable.[2]

But Grant, you may be thinking, *surely there are* some *instances where money motivation works?* Sure, for simple, straightforward tasks like manufacturing.[3] If someone just connects widget A with widget B in an assembly line, money motivation will probably work better in this instance. But if you want a team of people to work on more complicated concepts or tasks requiring creative thinking—if you want self-directed employees with an ownership mindset—it will take more than money to motivate them.

Millennials, defined as people born between 1981 and 1996, make up the largest percentage of the workforce in the United States—and they leave their jobs, on average, every 3.2 years. That statistic may confirm negative thoughts you have about millennials. You may even think, "That's why I don't want to hire millennials!" But did you know that everybody else, the non-millennial employ-

---

2   https://www.thebalancecareers.com/how-long-should-an-employee-stay-at-a-job-2059796

3   Dan Pink illustrates this fact beautifully in an RSA Animate YouTube video: https://youtu.be/u6XAPnuFjJc

ees who are the rest of the workforce, move on every 4.6 years?[4]

It's important for you, as a small business owner, to recognize that your team may stick around only three to five years before leaving to go work for another company, because you will face the high cost associated with finding new employees to replace those who leave. According to the Center of American Progress, it typically costs 20 percent of an employee's annual salary to replace that employee.[5] That means you'll pay somewhere between $6,000 and $15,000 every time you have to make a new hire—and that cost doesn't take into consideration the opportunity cost, the hours of your life, and the stress involved with filling the void left by the employee who quits.

The number one expense for most businesses is overhead related to employees. Way too many businesses are leaking money from their profit and loss statements related to either hiring and firing or employee performance as a whole. And that drain is frustrating. It erodes the trust you have in your team. It may even erode the trust you have in people altogether.

---

4   Bureau of Labor Statistics (https://www.bls.gov/news.release/tenure.nro.htm)

5   Center of American Progress (https://www.americanprogress.org/issues/economy/reports/2012/11/16/44464/there-are-significant-business-costs-to-replacing-employees/)

When you combine that cost with the experience of the other statistic we've talked about—that 88 percent of employees who are not working up to their potential—you see a team of people who are selfish, don't give it their best, and do not genuinely care about your business. That eats at you. You pour so much time, energy, and effort—not to mention money—into this person, and as soon as they start to get good at their job and start to make you some money, they're gone. You have to start over. At this point, you might be thinking, *Why bother? It's easier to just do it myself.*

I'm here to tell you that you *don't* have to do everything yourself. You don't have to be stuck performing every task; you can work on what you want, *when* you want. And you have value. You can take your product, service, and business to a completely new level that will make a much bigger impact and give you a whole lot more joy.

You just have to make a shift.

THE HIERARCHY OF MOTIVATION

You need to make a mindset shift, away from using money as the main motivation for your team, and focus on three new motivators: freedom, affirmation, and a unified purpose.

A lot of business owners feel like they can't afford to hire the best people because they can't pay the higher salaries that some of their bigger competitors can. "Grant," they say, "I can't get good talent because my comp plan doesn't compete well."

Studies tell us, however, that students graduating with not just bachelor's degrees but master's degrees and even doctorates are willing to take a significant pay cut in order to work for a company where they feel they get to do meaningful work or where they are part of a team pursuing something that matters together.[6] [7] [8]

Over 50 percent of currently employed people are looking for a new job—not because money's a problem, but because they don't feel like they're doing work that matters.[9] That statistic says that over half of your current staff—right now—is actively looking for another job because they don't think their current job makes a difference in the world. They're unable to attach meaning to what they're doing.

So what does matter?

---

6   https://www.fastcompany.com/90308995/i-took-a-huge-paycut-for-a-more-meaningful-job

7   https://www.cnbc.com/2018/06/27/nearly-9-out-of-10-millennials-would-consider-a-pay-cut-to-get-this.html

8   https://www.cnbc.com/2017/05/30/job-perks-prodding-millennials-to-work-for-less.html

9   https://www.forbes.com/sites/shephyken/2018/07/01/half-of-u-s-employees-are-actively-searching-for-a-new-job/#321f288d79c6

Article after article and study after study show the top five things the best talent is looking for, and every single time, compensation appears toward the bottom of the list—if it even makes it onto the list at all.[10] [11] [12] The top three things that people are looking for in their place of employment are things associated with autonomy or freedom, affirmation, and purpose.

FREEDOM

When people feel like they don't have freedom, or if they believe that their employer takes away their freedom rather than helping them gain more freedom in life, those people are going to feel trapped—and nobody works well when they feel trapped. It's unendurable over the long term. It limits productivity. Employees are not going to bring in their best ideas or work efficiently. Finally, tracking your employees—as traditional management says to implement—requires more time, energy, and effort from you as their manager, which takes away your freedom, too. Trusting your team to work as adults, however, makes things easier for everyone.

---

10 https://hbr.org/2018/02/people-want-3-things-from-work-but-most-companies-are-built-around-only-one

11 https://www.zenefits.com/blog/5-things-employees-value-more-than-salary/

12 https://www.inc.com/guides/2010/08/10-things-employees-want.html

AFFIRMATION

Lack of affirmation prevents employees from taking your desired actions because they don't know if what they're doing is right. It also limits growth. Employees can't grow in their abilities or become masters of their craft unless they are affirmed that they're going in the right direction—which helps your business as a whole grow as well.

PURPOSE

Finally, having a purpose around which your entire team is unified is statistically proven to attract the best talent and have the highest performing employees.

Throwing more money at this employment situation is not going to fix it. That's not going to motivate your team. The three elements that *will* effectively motivate them to become part of that 12 percent instead of where they currently are in the 88 percent are freedom, affirmation, and purpose.

MONEY MATTERS

So far, we've been talking about how money isn't the problem, but that doesn't mean that money doesn't *matter*.

Money is important. It's motivating; that's a fact. But it's not a primary motivator, not in the way that freedom, affirmation, and purpose are.

The reality is that people who are working in our society don't value their comp plan as much as you think they do. They value other things—things such as hearing they're doing a good job, being able to set their own schedules, and doing work that solves a problem—way more than their paycheck.

As I've mentioned before, Stewardship does home loans, insurance, and investments. One of the things we do very well is helping business owners manage their personal investments and also setting up their companies' 401(k) plans.

We manage the investments and personal finances for the owner of a small local business that has an *amazing* company culture. They are a model company, and the owner has set up his team's 401(k) plans with a 9 percent match—which is practically unheard of!

Despite the fact that this business owner's team *can* get up to a 9 percent match on their retirement plan, proof that money is not what makes the culture awesome, is that not all of the employees take advantage of that 9 percent match. When surveyed, the employees don't even mention that match as one of the reasons why they love working at this company.

They love working there because they have all kinds of freedom, they are affirmed like crazy, and there's a huge purpose that they are genuinely a family pursuing together.

I'm not saying your employees don't want money either. They do. I strongly believe in paying people fairly, in paying them what they're worth. You need to pay people enough so that money isn't an issue.

You're not asking them to volunteer—although I do want to point out that some of the most thriving entities in the world are nonprofits or businesses that have most of their workforce on a volunteer basis. That just serves as proof that money isn't the best motivator.

You can insert other motivators into your business that resonate better with your current employees and top talent. Not only will you get the most out of your team, but you're actually going to save a ton of money because you'll have better retention and see a direct impact on your profit and loss statement.

Again, money is important to your business—I'm not dispelling this. If you're not focusing on your P & L at some point, your business probably isn't going to be sustainable. Most business owners also worry about key performance indicators, figuring out return on investment, and analyzing data to make sure that what they're doing is efficient. That's wise.

But when it comes to your employees, money is not even one of the top three motivators for performance or remaining at a job.

So when it comes to managing people, you want to transition your mindset away from dollars and data and toward providing people with the things they really care about: Am I doing a good job? Am I appreciated? Does this job enhance the freedom I have in my life? Most importantly, when I show up to the office today and sit down at my desk, does what I'm doing even matter?

If the work is meaningless, why show up? If the employee feels like the task at hand is "because I have to," that's not going to work long term. But if they think, "It's because I want to!"—because what they're doing makes an impact on people and makes an impact on the world—then they're going to show up early, stay late, and do whatever is necessary to do the best job possible.

Providing freedom, affirmation, and a unified purpose attracts the best talent and ensures that your team will thrive.

REBUTTAL

Companies across the United States lose an estimated $450 billion to $550 billion every year due to lack of productivity and other costs related to having a poor company culture, according to a 2013 Gallup study on the state of the US workplace.[13]

This situation is not unique to you. A lot of people are facing this very same issue. You don't have to feel ashamed or like you're not good at finding the right people or even that you don't know how to motivate them. The truth is that our higher education institutes have not done a great job of preparing us to properly create a great company culture. That makes it really hard—but you can do this. You can learn how to change your company culture, not just to save money but to also make your company a better place to work.

You may be thinking, "Grant, you don't understand: I'm a for-profit company. I *do* come into the office to try to get money. I'm motivated by money, which means that everybody else is motivated by money, too. Money matters. Money's a big deal. The idea that money isn't the problem is false."

You're right; money does matter. It's number four on the list of what motivates people—after freedom, affirma-

---

13   https://www.gallup.com/services/176708/state-american-workplace.aspx

tion, and a unified purpose. I'm not saying that it's not important.

But why do people want more money?

When you break down money motivation, you can get to the real motivator. If an employee says, "I want more money so I can go on vacation," what does that actually mean? They want more money so they can have more *freedom*. If they say, "I want more money so I can drive a nice car, have a big house, and be seen as successful," what are they really saying? They want *affirmation*.

What if they say, "I want more money so I can provide more for my family and donate to this charitable cause?" Those are the *purpose*-driven people whom you want on your team!

What looks like money motivation actually points back to the three primary motivators the rest of this book will focus on: freedom, affirmation, and purpose. Money leads healthy, unselfish people to those three things— which is why it *is* important—but money is not actually the primary motivator for great employees.

Or you may be thinking, "Grant, this isn't going to work because I've had employees leave because I wasn't paying them enough. I'm having a really hard time finding new employees because the comp plan on my job offers is too low."

The real reason they left is because they got more money, and that money is going to allow them to have more freedom, affirmation, and a purpose. You just have to do a better job of providing that in your employment along with money, because when you can do all four, you attract the best talent. You have amazing retention and people don't leave. And you create that thriving company culture.

EVEN THE PEOPLE WHO HAVE LEFT ARE IN THE 12 PERCENT

I am extremely proud of my company's employment statistics. We have a high rate of retention, a low rate of bad hires, and awesome, tenured employees. At the beginning of this chapter, you learned about the first person to leave my company, but you may be wondering about the others. Surely, I've had people other than Mike quit, right?

Joey came to work for me as a mortgage person, doing loans. He was doing okay, but he is extremely creative and loves to create things. He didn't love the analytics, data, and spreadsheets so much. That just wasn't him. He left to start a company, Divinity Creative, doing graphic design. I affirmed him as he took this new path—and actually hired him to do some design for Stewardship.

Another employee who worked for me for a short time left to move across the country with her family when her husband got a job as a head coach at a college in another state. The funny thing is that when her husband eventually decided to leave coaching, he came to work for me—and he's one of my best employees. Because his wife had worked for me, he knew our company, and he's a great culture fit. (You'll get to read more about Marshall in chapter 3.)

Another assistant moved away when her husband got a job at a church in a different state. We recently had a remote position open up—a very basic, part-time position that could be done from home if the employee wanted to. The former assistant was one of the many applicants we got for that position. She loved the culture she worked for when she was here and jumped on the opportunity to be part of it again!

I also hired two other women who had similar motivations: they both wanted to be a mama someday, but they were unable to give birth to their own children. I supported them not only financially but also emotionally and along their journey of adoption. Both were able to adopt and ultimately decided to stay home with their children—but they bring their babies in so we can say hi and love on them!

Are you noticing a pattern here? The employees who

left did so as a result of changing life circumstances, not because they pursued better employment elsewhere. And, of course, I supported them as they made these transitions.

Brian was the only employee who was obviously not a good fit. He didn't appreciate the affirmation. He wasn't able to meet some of the goals, and he didn't properly go through the accountability process. He didn't thrive in the type of freedom I provide. And he didn't align much with the unified purpose. But the beauty of motivating this way, of having this framework in your culture, is that Brian came to me and said, "I probably need to get a new job."

There was no angst. How can you have angst toward someone who genuinely trusts you enough to give you the freedom you want? Someone who affirms you through everything you're doing and who gives you something to work toward? It doesn't create contentious relationships, which is beautiful. I helped him find another job, one with more structure that was a better fit for him personally, and now he's a source of referrals for our company. Don't gloss over that. Read it again—using this motivational hierarchy as part of creating an awesome company culture leads to *even employees who leave* becoming amazing referral sources who help me grow my business!

As we've established, doing everything yourself isn't

going to work. It's not sustainable. If you want to be efficient and you want to take your business to new levels, you have to focus on the super-important, high-level things you need to be doing.

This framework will allow you to have a team of people who are thriving while you focus on pushing your company to not only the level you currently want to push it to but even beyond what you can currently imagine.

But this book is not just about making a mindset shift toward giving your team freedom, affirmation, and purpose. We're going to talk about how to give them freedom, how to give them affirmation, and how to create a purpose and make sure that purpose is woven into everything you do.

You will begin to learn to apply these new motivators starting on the very next page. Chapter 2 is about freedom.

KEY TAKEAWAYS

- Money is necessary. It's important to consider your comp plan, but it is not *the most important* motivator. Employees rate freedom, affirmation, and having a purpose higher than a paycheck in their motivational hierarchy.

- Money motivation causes employees to switch jobs at an alarming rate, as they are always searching for the next thing that can pay them more money. This cycle is not good for employers—and it's not good for employees either.

- Using money as a primary motivator creates a culture of selfishness. Motivating through freedom, affirmation, and purpose, however, creates a team of self-directed employees who are innovative, take initiative, and do whatever is necessary to give your customers the best experience possible.

MY INTENTIONAL ACTIONS

CHAPTER 2

FREEDOM CREATES AN OWNERSHIP MENTALITY

We have unbelievably gorgeous weather in the spring in Arizona. In my opinion, it's the best place in the world to be.

We're also lucky because during the spring, half of the Major League Baseball teams play their spring training games here. Some days, you just want to be outside instead of cooped up in an office. So one day I told everyone, "I'm going to go work from the baseball game. Anybody want to come with? Let's go do it together!"

Going to a spring training game is inexpensive, laid-back, and a lot of fun. My team is equipped to work remotely from anywhere. We laid down blankets on the grass in the outfield and got a bunch of hot dogs, popcorn, and nachos. We laughed and joked on the way there and back.

Some people busted out their laptops and worked. Others worked from their phones. Some people didn't work at all and just enjoyed the sunshine and camaraderie. There was no pressure to get things done just because I was sitting there. I was there to love them, to make them feel happy. It was a day full of fun and smiles and laughter—not bad for a workday.

Later that day, I saw that my team posted about our day out on social media, showing pride in their jobs. Everyone else in the community sees how much Stewardship cares about its employees—and they think, "If they care about their employees this much, they probably care about their customers, too."

I do care about my employees—and our customers, too, of course—and one of the most important ways I can show them how much I care is by giving them *freedom*.

A TRAPPED TEAM

Wars have been waged throughout the history of time to create freedom. People want more freedom. We all desire it, so why don't we give it to our employees?

I believe, quite literally, that God created us with freedom in mind. That's why He gives us free will. A fundamental piece of how the earth functions exists around this concept of free will. So if that free will is removed from work, people feel trapped—and nobody works well when they feel trapped. It's not viable, and it limits productivity.

Many managers, employers, and small business owners (who are often one and the same) have a difficult time making the mindset shift toward trusting their employees. Without that trust, employees don't feel free.

And even with all your amazing success—with everything you've done to build your business this far, to get all the clients and customers you have, and to establish your company in a competitive industry—you might discover that you have a difficult time trusting people, too. That may be from having employees before who didn't work out. Maybe they watched the clock instead of being self-directed employees who were motivated to work hard toward a goal.

Whatever the reason, it is important to understand that you won't be able to properly give your team freedom unless you do trust them.

I know that's hard to hear. This next part might be even harder, but you need to hear it: if you don't trust your employees, that's not their problem; it's your problem. Trust is not earned—it's given; and you're the one who needs to give that trust. If someone on your team isn't worthy of your trust, it is again a "you" problem because you hired them.

But the good news is, you have two options: you can either start trusting your team, or if they're not trustworthy, you can hire new employees whom you can trust. Your team should have the freedom to work for your customers, care for them, and serve them.

MICROMANAGERS ARE NOT WISE MANAGERS

If you don't trust your employees, you micromanage them, and they don't feel free.

Have you heard yourself saying any of the following recently?

- "Did you do this today?"
- "Here's how you have to do this."
- "I would have done that differently."
- "Let me just do it. Give me the mouse/keyboard/ phone."

Sound familiar?

When employees don't have your trust, it prevents any freedom, creativity, or ability for that person to grow into a self-directed employee.

We all want self-directed employees, but they rarely start off self-directed from day one. They have to grow into that role because they have to learn to work within your organization and under your leadership. They need to become self-directed toward your purpose, toward your business, toward the best way to work for you.

Micromanagement, however, prevents employees from becoming self-directed. It trains your team not to perform any tasks until they receive cues from you. When you say, "Hey, do these things today," what happens when your employees finish those things? They sit around and twiddle their thumbs and wait for you to tell them the next thing to do.

A self-directed employee, on the other hand, understands the unified purpose and says, "I'm going to do anything and everything I can think of in my day to meet that purpose. I'm going to accomplish tasks without my boss having to tell me what to do, because I have the freedom to act on my own accord."

The truth is that none of us truly *want* to micromanage our employees. It takes way too much time and energy. If

I tried to micromanage each of my employees, I wouldn't be able to get anything else done. I wouldn't be able to spend my time on what's most valuable. I wouldn't be able to fulfill my role as a business owner and CEO. My freedom would be taken away, too.

When you don't trust your employees, you are stuck either doing everything yourself or micromanaging everyone around you. You're unable to escape from the day-to-day. Your business becomes completely dependent on you, every day and every moment. Performance takes a dive as soon as you're out of the office. That means you can't turn your phone off. You can't leave the office. You can't just *take a vacation.*

But you know what happens when you *do* trust your team and when your employees *do* have freedom? They get things done. They perform. They do their jobs and meet your unified purpose *whether you are in the office or not.* My team breaks records when I'm out of the office, because they know what needs to be done and they do it, no hand-holding involved.

SET THEM FREE

Let's look at ways employees often feel trapped and what you can do to ensure your team has the freedom they need in order to thrive.

SCHEDULES

Harvard Business Review concluded that very few people can be in a state of high concentration for more than four or five days in a row. On top of that, in this study, they said that the human brain has a hard time sustaining more than four or five extremely productive hours in a day.[14]

Everybody thinks they have to work forty hours a week, but the study shows that you have a limited number of peak performance hours in a week—and it's not forty. The whole idea that we're supposed to work forty hours a week was created during the manufacturing era, around how the machine manufacturing process worked. The man who came up with the forty-hour workweek analyzed his machinery and determined that they operated most efficiently at approximately forty hours per week. So this schedule was never created for humans or how *we* are designed to work most effectively.

According to David Rock's book *Your Brain at Work*, that number is more like six peak performance hours in an entire week. Beyond that, you get four to five hours a day of productive time, no more than four or five days a week. To expect more than that is unrealistic.

These studies serve to debunk the mentality of the work, work, work, grind, grind, grind. Do people have the abil-

---

14   https://hbr.org/2011/05/being-more-productive

ity to work and grind and go hard for certain lengths of time? Of course. You've probably done it yourself. But it's not sustainable. Most of that grinding and working has been drudgery—not your extremely productive peak performance.

Understanding this truth is just step one. Part of the freedom that people need in order to be their most productive is the freedom to choose when it's best for them to tap into their peak performance.

You can give people freedom to have that really productive time in the four or five hours that work best for them. Give them the freedom to find their circadian rhythm, whether they're most productive in the morning, middle of the day, or later in the afternoon. We're all wired differently.

Some people think you have to wake up at 4:30 a.m., when the sun's still down, to get anything done. That's exactly the opposite of me. I wake up about eight o'clock every day. Some people would think that I'm lazy, but my peak performance hours are in the evenings after my kids are in bed.

I have the freedom to do that because I own my own business. So how cool would it be if your employees had the freedom to be able to find their own peak performance time?

Now, I'm not saying you have to give all your employees complete autonomy to work anytime within the twenty-four-hour day. At the very least, though, you should allow them to gain an understanding of when they are most productive within the workday or within their scheduled hours—and then give them the freedom to choose to do their most important work during that time.

We've all heard about the 80/20 rule. Well, here 20 percent of the time in your week is where you're going to come up with 80 percent of your productivity. You want to give your team the freedom to find out where their 20 percent is, encourage them, and create a culture and an environment that leans into that fact. You now know that they can't be kicking ass 100 percent of the time. The forty-hour workweek simply isn't how our brains are wired. So help them figure out where that 20 percent is and really set them up for success.

BREAKS

How stupid and inefficient is it when bathroom breaks are scheduled? What if you don't have to go? Do you go sit there, just because it's on the schedule, instead of being treated like a responsible adult who can manage their own time? It doesn't make any sense.

We're not working in a coal mine. We don't have to tell

people, "You get fifteen minutes for break." Then, if they're two seconds over that, "Let's go. Pick up your shovel and pickax."

Telling somebody when to take a break, how long they can have for lunch, or how often they can go to the bathroom is going to make them feel trapped. It gives them zero freedom.

And you don't have to do that. You have the opportunity to give your team the freedom to take the breaks they want.

(I know that right now, you're already thinking, "Grant, I can't do that. People will take advantage of the freedom." Just wait. Remember that I address all the common rebuttals at the end of the chapter. For now, make note of your comment and keep reading.)

Everybody needs different amounts of time. They have different reactions to what's going on in the day. As their manager, you won't necessarily know everything your team is going through. Did they get a good night's sleep last night? Or were they tossing and turning because a spouse or child is sick? Were they able to leave the house with encouragement and vigor? Or are they going through a season of additional stress in their life?

Allowing your employees the freedom to structure their

workday helps the ups and downs of life to become smoother. You can't underestimate how much that helps your team—or how much *value* they will find in having that freedom.

I have some people on my team who need only a five-minute break here or there. They don't want to take a full fifteen minutes because it messes up the rhythm of what they're working on. Other people need more time. I trust them all to know themselves, to know their own bodies, and to do what works best for them. They know what they need to pursue our purpose effectively and efficiently—and break records doing it!

When we feel like we have to focus on how long our team is taking a break, then we as managers get pissed when they do take a longer break. Someone could be a very high-performing employee, but if they go five minutes over on their break, we get irritated and it ruins our day.

But why? So what if they take longer? That doesn't do us any harm. We have to let go of that micromanagement and just trust people that they're going to use the restroom or eat lunch or take a break whenever they need to.

When I worked in a sea of cubicles as a credit card collector, I would often have very emotional phone calls with people. I remember a big win, when somebody paid in full. It was a great call, but it took a lot out of me to engage with this person, work hard with them, and essentially make the sale happen.

After that, I couldn't just go on to the next call. I needed a break to renew myself and ensure I could be my best on the next call. But I looked at my watch and saw that my next break wasn't scheduled for forty-seven minutes. My manager had zero leeway for unscheduled breaks, so I pretended that I had to go to the bathroom just so I could splash water on my face and breathe for a bit.

Think about that: In order to continue producing at a high level, I knew that I needed to refresh. But my manager didn't allow me the freedom to do that, so I was forced to compromise my integrity and say that I needed to use the restroom, just so I could continue to operate at the level I expected of myself. How shortsighted is that?

You might think that employees who take the shortest breaks are the most productive, but that isn't true. There was a study done that required people to take a break every twenty minutes.[15] And it wasn't just to stop working for a minute or just look up from their task. No, every twenty minutes they had to get on their personal social

---

15 https://www.inc.com/amy-vetter/how-working-in-25-minute-sprints-makes-you-sharper-more-productive.html

media, watch a video they wanted to watch unrelated to their work, or use their work computer for personal use.

The study found that the number of minutes those employees spent working in a day went down, which makes sense. More breaks means less production time on the clock...but the amount they were able to produce dramatically increased. Because they were able to raise the level of production per minute, they were able to produce more in a single day—even when the total work time was reduced. Starting to make sense now?

Another study done by Happify, which appears in the book *The Happiness Advantage* by Shawn Achor, shows that allowing employees to take breaks whenever they want—no scheduled lunches, just eating whenever they want to eat, taking a break whenever they need one— leads to a 30 percent higher level of focus when they are working. The brain activity of the study participants was higher, which led to increased efficiency. They had over 50 percent higher levels of creativity, which means they were better able to solve problems. And they were 46 percent less likely to call in sick or miss work.[16]

Don't miss that fact. It's important to repeat: people who had more freedom in the workday were half as likely to miss work as everyone else. That's huge! Giving freedom

16   Shawn Achor, *The Happiness Advantage* (New York: Currency, 2010).

around breaks not only means that you, as an employer, are going to save money on sick time, but you're also going to have your team there in the office more often.

TIME OFF

Vacation time and sick time is another area where employees can feel trapped without freedom—and it's just one more thing you have to track and manage as an employer. How many hours per week or month do you or someone on your staff spend logging hours worked, time-off requests, PTO, and vacation time? How many payroll systems or technological applications do you pay for to ensure that all of these pieces are being managed correctly? Ask.com claims that its unlimited vacation policy saves fifty-two HR staff hours every year![17]

I don't have to deal with any of that! Not the expenses and, more importantly, not the wasted time spent dealing with it all.

It's frustrating when people call in sick, but as I previously mentioned, many of those sick days aren't being taken due to true illness. Employees are calling in because they need a day to relax or unwind because their current work environment is too rigid. The lack of freedom in their

---

17   https://www.shrm.org/resourcesandtools/hr-topics/benefits/pages/unlimited-pto.aspx

workday wears on them, so they require more time away from the office.

My team can leave whenever they want. I don't track their sick time. I don't track their vacation time. In fact, as we've established, I don't track their time at all. They have the freedom to come and go whenever they want. I know, I know. "Grant, that won't work for me because *reasons*." I've heard it all before. Don't worry, the rebuttal section is coming, and I'll address your concerns there.

This level of freedom positively impacts the quality of my life as a manager as well. I don't have to track when people are taking breaks, how long they take for lunch, or when they're coming and going. I don't track any of that, because it doesn't matter. What matters is how they're pursuing our unified purpose—and as long as they can accomplish that and produce as expected, I quite literally don't care if they work one hour throughout the year or all 365 days.

Sound crazy? Let me give you an extreme example to prove my point:

Employee A works 365 days a year but produces only $100 of *net* profit for your business. Employee B works just *one day a year*, but in that day they produce $1,000,000 of net profit for your business. Which employee would you choose?

The obvious—and overly simplified—answer is employee B. Why? Because it's not about the hours the employee works; it's about the production of those hours.

This practice creates the sense of freedom that all human beings long for and gives employees time to be with their families and pursue the things that matter most to them. That, therefore, means that their employment supports the things they care about—and that's a big deal. If their job and their boss support the things that are most important to them, those employees are going to think about their jobs in a completely different light.

Multiple studies have also shown that when you don't track sick or vacation time, when you give it to employees on an unlimited basis, *they take far less time off than when it is tracked.*[18] [19]

Think about it. We've all heard people say things like, "Oh yeah, my boss told me I still have x number of vacation days to take, so I have to use them or I'll lose them."

I don't track that, so that conversation never happens, which means my employees aren't looking for a reason to take time off just to use up their vacation days or PTO.

---

18 https://www.zenefits.com/blog/unlimited-pto/

19 https://www.inc.com/magazine/201606/minda-zetlin/unlimited-vacation-benefits.html

That conversation goes beyond vacation and sick days. Giving employees the freedom to take the time they need creates a connection and a relationship between you and your team that most employers completely miss.

Our conversation goes more like this:

EMPLOYEE: "Hey, I'm not going to be here next week. I'm going on vacation!"

ME: "Great! Where are you going?"

EMPLOYEE: "We're going to the beach with the kids."

ME: "That's going to be so fun! Your kids are going to have a blast. Oh, you should try this coffee shop! I tried it when I was there, and it was great."

Now you're having a conversation about their life. After we've had that moment of connection, I continue:

ME: "Well, you know how it is here: it's all about meeting our purpose of loving people through finances. So are you going to be able to get everything done? Are people going to be loved through finances while you're gone?"

EMPLOYEE: "Yeah, I've talked to team member A and they're covering my sales duties. Team member B is helping on the administrative duties. Plus, I plan to bring my laptop to stay on top of stuff from time to time. We shouldn't miss a beat!"

And that's all it is. But because I was able to have that first conversation, it goes much better. It creates a connection; it creates unity. Giving them that freedom lets your employees know that you genuinely care about them.

SOCIAL ENGAGEMENT

Your team will be able to produce on higher levels if they have social engagement at work. They will connect and pursue a purpose together. But social engagement can't happen without freedom.

The dumbest thing in the world to me is when bosses say not to use your cell phone at work or not to use the computer for personal stuff. When I hear that, it's like, "Are you freaking kidding me?" Our lives are on our cell phones! What happens if an employee's kid gets sick at school and they're worried about that? That's all they're going to be thinking about because they can't check in for updates. That's ridiculous to me. Everybody has a life outside of work. Let that life happen—and encourage it.

An employee shouldn't have to sneak onto social media to find something to laugh at and get a dopamine hit in their brain. That's a good thing—and that's what social media has been designed to deliver. I'm not going to take away this thing that sends dopamine—which is important to productivity, creativity, well-being, and happiness. I'm going to encourage that!

You might see people standing around the water cooler, chatting or telling jokes. When they have the freedom of social engagement, you won't see them stop talking and scurry back to their desks when you walk by. In fact, you can join the water cooler talk, engage with them, and make that break longer.

The next thing you know, it seems like you just spent twenty-five minutes doing nothing—but it wasn't nothing. That was high-quality social engagement, which will genuinely create a better level of productivity right after the social engagement as well as later on.

My team works really hard. They serve our community in unbelievable ways. The truth is, to serve people at high levels and have amazing customer service, you have to take on more than most people do. So I have to take on a higher level of creativity to make opportunities for more social engagement. I set up a projector in the break room where people can play video games, unwind, and engage with one another. And, of course, they have the freedom to do so whenever they want. These things allow them to reset so they can maintain those extremely high levels of production.

You can create an environment where social engagement happens and is encouraged in word and deed. The water cooler isn't always a literal water cooler anymore. So what's going to be that thing or area where everybody congregates to make jokes and talk about things?

Social engagement doesn't always mean telling jokes and playing video games. It means people in the office becoming friends, talking about the things they really care about, and building deep, quality relationships. My team members hang out with one another outside of work, and I *love* that. It means that they truly care about one another—and my culture allowed for that to happen. Think that doesn't matter? Wrong. Remember when an employee needed to get help covering some vacation time? That happens with joy in my office because our coworkers care so much about one another. They're happy to have a friend's back!

Our company has also created a place where the whole team has the freedom to bring their spouses and kids to work. The environment is family friendly, so kids feel like they are welcomed. They don't have to worry about being quiet or not running around. We give them high fives when we see them coming! It's an environment where everyone is free to be themselves.

You might think it's crazy for a financial institution to allow such unprofessional activity. What happens if a customer sees that? Won't they lose respect for the business? Quite the opposite! Our customers love seeing that the office is a family-friendly environment. They have families, too, after all.

I'm not saying our office is a day care. Employees don't bring their kids to work every day, but families know that they're welcome. This does amazing things for employee performance as well. Their spouses and children feel valued. They have a sense of pride about what their husband or wife or mother or father do for a living. All of this means that your employees have people at home who support their employment—and it creates more fans for your business!

Imagine, for a moment, overhearing other people—people who don't even work for you—talking about how great your business is.

FRIEND: What does your husband do for a living?

EMPLOYEE'S SPOUSE: He works for this great company. It's an amazing place, and I'm so proud of him.

FRIEND: Does he like working there?

EMPLOYEE'S SPOUSE: He loves his work, and we love

it, too. We can come visit him at the office anytime we want, and we feel so welcome there.

FRIEND: Oh wow, that's so unique. It sounds great! And your kids like it, too?

EMPLOYEE'S KID: Yeah, it's the best!

That only happens if they have the freedom to create a community where awesome things happen. When it does, it's going to bleed outside of the office—and your company is going to become a place that other people want to get involved with.

I no longer ever have a job search where I have to find people to submit résumés. If we have an opening, I put it on social media once and we get an overwhelming response because everyone wants to work here. The freedom we give people is attractive. People want to be part of this community. Even more, they want to be a part of this family!

TAKE ACTION

Most classical management books create so many policies and procedures that make things super-complicated because they are not based on trusting people.

One of the cool things about freedom is that your job and

your life become easier, too. Take a look at all the policies and procedures you have in place and ask yourself, "Which of these are complicated for my team and require more time for me to manage?" And then, "How much of that can I remove?"

What can you simplify, for your employees and for yourself, that will give all of you more freedom?

Part of the reason you want to be the boss and own your own business is because you can come and go as you please at work. You can take lunches whenever you want, use your phone for personal calls, and no one's going to tell you otherwise.

So how can you as the owner model the freedom that you want your employees to have?

If a really cool movie trailer comes out that everyone is interested in, maybe you can invite everyone to watch it in your office. If you feel like you need a long break today, be open and honest about that. "Hey, I'm struggling. I'm going across the street to get a frozen yogurt. Anyone want to come with?"

If you're going on vacation, talk about that, too. "I'm going to be out of the office for a week, but here's how I'm still going to get my stuff handled."

Bring your kids into the office and let them act like kids. Better yet, when your employees bring in their kids, encourage them to act like kids. Have candy at your desk and cheer as you give it away. (But make sure they ask mom or dad first!)

Model the behavior, live it, and intentionally show that you're living it. The best intentions require intentional actions. You might have the best intention to give your staff freedom, but it requires intentional actions, over and over again, consistently, in order for those best intentions to be received and lived out.

All the freedoms I have in place at my office are because I believe they're going to help meet our unified purpose of loving people through finances. To love someone well, you have to love them on their terms. You have to meet them where they are. You may think, "Sounds cool, Grant, but what does that actually look like?"

How do my employees know what it looks like to love people through finances? It starts with me loving them. If they ever wonder how to love our customers, they can start by treating our customers the same way I treat them. I cannot genuinely say that I'm going to love my employees with everything I've got unless I also give them the freedom and trust to do so.

AN OWNERSHIP MENTALITY

One of your biggest frustrations is probably that your employees aren't doing things the way you would do them. They act like they are checking things off a task list rather than taking a genuine, holistic interest in the entirety of a project or the company. There's a good chance they look at the clock more than they look for problems to solve.

Giving them freedom creates an ownership mentality, which helps get your team in the right mindset to do things the way you want them to.

Following the steps listed in this chapter saves a crazy amount of time because you're not telling them how to do things or giving them cues of when and how to work. It simplifies the life of everyone because doing this right naturally builds in self-accountability in your team. That creates freedom for you, too.

You may be wondering what freedoms to give and how to properly implement them. The best freedoms are the ones that are in line with your unified purpose, which should be simple and clearly communicated. (You'll get clear on it yourself in chapter 4!)

Your unified purpose is going to look different than mine, so the freedoms for your company, for your team, are going to be different, too. For the most part, I let my employees come and go as they please. I trust them to manage their own workday, and I provide opportunities for them to relax and unwind in the office with things such as video games, cold-brew coffee on tap, and Netflix and social media on their work computers. I give everyone the freedom to work remotely and trust them to take time when they need it—but to make sure work still gets done when they're gone.

Some of the above may not work for you, and that's okay! You don't have to have the same policies and procedures that I have. But if you want to have the same level of trust I have with my team, that trust and their ownership mentality come about through freedoms, whatever freedom looks like for you and your team.

REBUTTAL

Your biggest rebuttal here is likely to be internal. "Grant, if I give my team freedom, they're going to run amok. If I don't have any boundaries in place, they aren't going to be efficient. They're not going to work hard. They're going to socialize too much and waste time. I'm not going to pay people to just do whatever they want, willy-nilly, whenever they want."

It may seem like my company is limitless freedom, but

it does have structure. The human brain operates well with guidance and within structure. But most employers go way beyond what is necessary. I understand that you need to have boundaries, but what freedoms can you give within those limits? Where can you give trust, still within the boundaries, to allow for higher production?

Harvard Business Review has concluded after various studies that the most profitable workplaces, those that have the highest performing employees, are the ones where social relationships are heightened and employees have the freedom to engage with one another. If you want high-performing employees, you have to intelligently and intentionally give your team freedom and social engagement.

If your mindset is that you're not paying people to socialize, then your company is not going to be as profitable or have as high employee performance as it could, according to *Harvard Business Review*. Most managers look at employees hanging out together and see money flying out the window. When you shift your mindset and understand the truth, however, watching your team engage socially should remind you of a battery being recharged. You know that more energy and better effort is forthcoming from those employees!

The external struggle is, "I don't really know how to

give these freedoms, and I don't know if I can trust my employees."

Hire only people whom you trust, or starting trusting them. See how they do with freedom. This is an excellent opportunity for you to see who is trustworthy and who isn't by giving them some freedom and seeing what they do with it. Those who thrive with their new freedom are proving their value to you and your company. Those who struggle are showing that they may not be the best fit for your team.

Remember, it takes a lot of energy and effort to limit freedom, and it costs money. Is your time best spent sitting in a watchtower, ensuring that your team does what they need to do? Think what you can do with your time if you don't have to constantly keep a watchful eye over people. How much more efficient would your day be if you had a team of self-directed employees who had the freedom to pursue your company's purpose in the best way possible? What entrepreneurial ideas and actions could you take? How much more would the company be able to grow if you had that time available to focus on big-picture endeavors?

If you don't know how to implement this, start a little at a time. Genuinely put yourself in your employees' shoes and walk through the experiences your team goes through at work. Which of those experiences frustrate you? Which require a lot of effort and energy? Where do you feel a lack of trust? Write those things down and make small changes to address those areas.

You'll find out that certain freedoms you tried to give just didn't work out—and that's okay. Try giving freedom somewhere else. It's a process to learn what type of freedom works best for your management style and in your company. The bottom line here is that freedom needs to be intentionally and intelligently given.

Freedom is the first motivator in this book, but it's only the third most motivating force for the human brain in our society. There are more pieces of the puzzle to have a thriving team. The next chapter looks at the second piece of the motivational hierarchy: affirmation.

KEY TAKEAWAYS

- Giving your employees freedom to do their jobs however they work best does not set you up to be taken advantage of. It sets you up to have a successful team of people who do whatever it takes to get the job done.

- If you don't trust your employees, that is a "you" problem—and it *is* a problem. You hired your team, so you need to start trusting them. Give your trust freely and watch your employees perform better than you anticipated.

- If you don't allow your team to choose how to use their time while at the office, they will not become the high-performing, self-directed producers you want. Giving employees this type of freedom, however, fosters an environment that encourages the ownership mentality of employees to go above and beyond when solving problems. Why? Because they are trusted and *free* to do so.

MY INTENTIONAL ACTIONS

....

....

....

....

....

....

....

....

....

....

....

CHAPTER 3

AFFIRMATION CREATES CONFIDENCE

In traditional employee reviews, goals are set for employees—and those goals are often set just outside what is possible for that person to achieve.

When I performed these reviews with Mike (the employee you met in the introduction and chapter 1 who left and returned twice to Stewardship), I looked at his average performance. He could typically close x number of loans in a month when he was performing at his peak, so I set a goal for him to close y number of loans—more than he had ever reached before—and I told him that if he hit the goal, he would get a financial incentive.

The next month, he closed x number of loans again, which was actually a great number, but I still had to tell him that he didn't hit his goal. Month after month, no matter how well he did and how much I profited, that goal was set up to be just out of his reach. And every time we got together to do performance reviews, he just took it on the chin. "You had this goal, but you didn't meet it—again."

Even though I was completely thrilled with his performance, Mike thought, "I'm not good at my job. I'm terrible at closing loans. I suck!"

And, effectively, that's what I was telling him. The only information I gave him was, "Here's this goal that I know you can't meet, but I'm going to put it on paper anyway, because that's what everybody tells us to do in management school."

Next thing I know, Mike came into the office with his head down. He dressed differently, barely tucking his shirt in because he had no confidence. When he talked with people, he hesitated and even *sounded* different because every word was infused with the feeling that he just wasn't good at his job.

In those moments, I was a terrible leader. I knew what I was doing setting those goals outside of his reach—I was doing what all the management books said—but I didn't even realize what I *wasn't* doing to give value to my employee: I didn't affirm him in any way.

HOW AM I DOING?

Three of the biggest poisons to a company culture are uncertainty, lack of leadership, and lack of confidence.

Employees give up forty hours or more every week, and they work hard even if they do it for money-motivated reasons. And at the end of the day, we all just want to know *how* we're doing—especially the high achievers. If you want top talent, you have to let them know even *more*.

As your team works every day, every week, every month, they're wondering, "Am I doing this right? Is this what I'm supposed to be doing?" They're waiting for a leader to help them see where they're going—and exactly how they're going to get to this place. Lack of this leadership, combined with uncertainty, means that employees are left floundering, unsure of what direction to take.

Similarly, a lack of confidence prevents people from taking the actions they need to take. Without confidence, employees won't step out from their set roles to do what needs to be done. They may avoid difficult tasks. They don't look for problems and take actions to solve them because they don't believe they have that ability. Or they may be too unsure to act on a creative urge that could take the business to a completely different level.

On the other hand, a study performed by *Harvard Business Review* shows that optimistic employees outperform their peers by 66 percent.[20] Is this because of their sunny, "look on the bright side" attitude? No. It's because those employees have confidence, which is one of the biggest commodities of high-performing employees. In this study, high-stress environments were created, and the people who were able to perform at a high level—not just do the job but exceed expectations—all had confidence.

Don't think that study is accurate? Evaluate your current team. I bet that your highest producing employees have higher levels of confidence. Conversely, lower producing employees have lower levels of confidence. Now think of yourself. When you have achieved high results, did you have confidence? Of course. And the better results you got, the more confidence followed—allowing you to continue to achieve more and more.

Fortunately, you already have a tool that you can use to eliminate your employees' uncertainty about how they're doing, give them the leadership they desire, and build their confidence—and that tool is *affirmation.*

---

20   https://hbr.org/2019/03/the-financial-upside-of-being-an-optimist

We have two words in the English language that, when put together, become extremely important: "I am." The words after that, when we say, "I am *this*," are called self-talk, and our self-talk becomes what we believe about ourselves.

As an employer, you want your team's self-talk to give them confidence: "I am great at this. I am loved. I am helpful. I am important. I am valuable." When they say those things, they'll perform better. Ultimately, you want them to say, "I am really good at my job." When they believe that, you'll see your employees act with confidence and kick butt because of it.

But you're not in your employees' heads, so how can you affect their self-talk, confidence, and performance? By using the two words that are even *more* important than "I am"—"*You are.*"

Affirmations are what you say after the words "You are." A leader who says, "You are missing your goals again for the third straight month because you did things the wrong way," is going to have a completely different team from a leader who says, "You are important; you just made x amount of revenue for the company." Or, "You are good at your job; you just helped us meet our unified purpose in y way."

The words you use to tell your team how they're doing

can bolster their own self-talk, making it more cohesive and helping it stick around longer in their heads.

CONFIDENCE TO PERFORM

Statistics and experience tell us that confidence helps people perform when the pressure is on. When you need performance the most, when you need your team to do well because you're depending on them, they need confidence.

When employees get off the phone with a customer or engage in a project, we often see one of two things happen: the first employee hangs up the phone and appears defeated. They say, "Oh, crap. That conversation didn't go very well. That's not what I wanted to happen." Their self-talk may become, "I'm just not good at this." The second employee, however, finishes the call and claps, saying, "Yeah! I did it!"

We want this second scenario. We want our teams to act with confidence, to know that they just performed at a high level, and to cheer for themselves and their teammates. When they experience more of those moments, employees reinforce that feeling so that they're going to perform only at those heights.

I played basketball in college. When I was a freshman on

the court, a lot of my thoughts were, "I'm new, I'm slower, I can't make this shot. Don't pass me the ball. I'm not going to score." And because I didn't have confidence, I didn't perform well. I'd turn the ball over and miss the shots. I didn't think it mattered if I fouled out because I didn't believe my team really needed me out there. My self-talk was, "I'm not that important to the team."

But then I changed my self-talk. I started telling myself, "I'm the best player on the court." If someone fouled me and I went to the free-throw line, I thought, "Ha ha, you messed up. These are free points for me!"

In the last year of my career, I was shooting over 90 percent from the free-throw line, and I was one of the best defenders on the team. I simply believed that no one would be able to consistently score on me. Nothing else changed. My abilities didn't really increase. Sure, I practiced, but to be honest, my knees and back got worse throughout my career. I was more athletic when I was a freshman. But despite my lesser physical abilities, I was a much better player at the end of my career just because I had that confidence.

The same thing happens at work all the time.

Just the other day, a prospective customer called one of the financial advisors. This person called with an *atti-*

tude. You know the customer I'm talking about—the guy who has his guard up, looking for a fight. The person who wants to bully his way through the conversation, forcing everything to be on his terms.

Most people would be intimidated by this type of customer. He thrives on adding fear and uncertainty—and removing confidence. But rather than sheepishly and awkwardly deliberating about terms and investment returns, the advisor on the call had all the confidence in the world. He listened well, asked questions, listened some more, and then talked about the solutions we have to meet the customer's goals.

My team member had a clear understanding of our unified purpose, and he'd had previous successful experiences loving even the most difficult customers. He was able to respond to this customer with authority and empathy, having the confidence to exude our mantra: "We're wise, and we love you."

The customer had confidence in the advisor and that his goals would be met so he could have the financial future he wants. Not only did we win the business, we now have a raving fan!

HOW TO USE AFFIRMATION

When affirmations are done correctly, you're never waiting months for a performance review to tell your team how they're doing. They know how they're doing because you tell them right away. If they need to correct something about how they're doing their job, you correct it on the spot, in the moment, or as close to it as possible.

Affirming in the moment gives your team the feedback they need to get better at their jobs as they work at it each day and each week. And it encourages them to repeat the action or behavior that gets results.

Generally speaking, leaders do a poor job of keeping track of all the awesome things their team is doing. But everyone can keep track of awesome stories and use them to affirm others. I'm constantly gathering data, listening, helping, and talking to my team about how to improve on a daily basis, because that's what they want. That's what everybody wants.

STEP ONE: COLLECT AFFIRMATIONS

There's a moment in every phone call, every interaction, or at least every day where your employee did something right. There is always something you can affirm.

Affirmation goes beyond saying small things like, "Hey,

you're really good," or "You did this great thing." You can do that only so many times before eventually it falls on deaf ears. And if you keep saying the same things over and over again, it comes across as disingenuous. As mentioned in a previous chapter, it matters to your team that you show them that you genuinely care for them.

Start collecting the data of all the great things your team is doing—anything from meeting your purpose well, completing a great task, having a good statistic, engaging in a great conversation, or receiving a referral or compliment from somebody else.

Write down anything and everything positive. Have a note on your phone or computer or even a blank page in a notebook where you write down every time an employee does something awesome. That way, your affirmations will be targeted and specific.

Now, instead of simply saying, "Great job," you can say, "Hey, I listened to that call you had, and it was really great! When you asked the customer follow-up questions to get more specific on her goals, it helped her feel loved—and it helped you respond with a better solution. *That* is loving people through finances. Well done!"

See the difference?

STEP TWO: BE INTENTIONAL

I've said it before and I'll say it again: the best intentions require the most intentional actions. You might have the best intentions to be the most encouraging boss ever, but far too few of us actually take that action. No one intends to be a jerk or for their spouse not to know that they're awesome, right? Nobody is intentionally an absentee parent or silent boss who gives no direction—so why do some managers leave their employees guessing about their performance?

All of us have the best intentions for our employees and their whole families to love their job, and that takes some intentional action. Write down the affirmations and then share them with your team member.

Schedule time in your calendar to affirm people. Take fifteen or thirty minutes to walk around the office, give high fives, tell people they're awesome and doing their jobs right, and read them an affirmation you listed over the past day.

My team always tells me, "Grant, I love it when you come out of your office to talk with us. It's so encouraging, and I feel fired up to keep going."

Doing this doesn't cost any money, and your team will love it!

STEP THREE: MAKE SURE YOUR TEAM KNOWS HOW THEY'RE DOING

I love to have living, breathing scoreboards so my team always has the answer to "How am I doing?"

We all use some sort of technology in our jobs, and you can get that technology to integrate with performance trackers or even Excel or Google Sheets.

I make sure that each employee has a URL that links to a scoreboard that is constantly updated based on how they're doing at their job. They can look at it throughout their day. Some employees utilize it more than others, but the competitive ones love seeing their numbers grow as the day, week, or month progresses.

We also have these scoreboards for everyone to see how the whole team is doing. That way, I can publicly encourage certain employees in front of their peers, which creates a culture of encouragement. It's not uncommon to have one employee encourage another based on the awesome work they are doing. Or better, have one employee ask another how they're achieving those results. These public scoreboards can generate a lot of collaboration.

Sadly, not many businesses do this or do it well. But having these scoreboards in place removes that uncertainty around "Am I doing a good job?" Employees can see that they've done something right or they got a win right away. That affirmation then builds confidence. When they know they're doing it right, they can keep going.

STEP FOUR: GET CREATIVE

There are a thousand different ways you can affirm somebody to let them know they're doing a fantastic job.

I keep a cabinet in our office filled with thank-you cards, and every so often, I take time to fill them out. If I'm going to be out of the office, I'll write down the affirmations and leave them for my employees. Sometimes I mail it to their house so they get something nice in the mail while I'm gone.

We have a Slack channel called Loving People Well, and anytime a customer fills out a review about our company, it automatically goes to that Slack channel so we can all have a conversation and celebrate it together.

As a business owner, I'm always asked to go to different galas and events for nonprofits. If we get a gift bag, we'll save it for someone on the team. If there's a silent auction, my wife will bid on as much cool stuff as she can, and we never take any of it home. We give it to the employees and tell them how awesome they are and show them that we were thinking of them.

Almost all of us have some sort of social media presence, and that's the perfect place to share how your employees are doing with the world. If you don't follow me on Instagram yet, go ahead and do that now: @grantbotma. I routinely make a post about one of my employees, so you can check them out to see what this looks like in action.

Giving a shout-out about the awesome things your team is doing shows your pride in them! Their friends and family can see how much you appreciate their hard work.

STEP FIVE: AFFIRM YOUR TEAM IN FRONT OF PEOPLE WHO ARE IMPORTANT TO THEM

Another great way to affirm your team is doing so in public—but it's even more meaningful when you praise someone in front of the people who are most important to them. You'll want to intentionally affirm your employees in front of their family every opportunity you get.

If kids come into the office, one of the first things I do is get on the kid's level, look them in the eye, and say, "Is that your mommy over there? Did you know that your mommy is really good at her job? She did this amazing thing..." I basically tell the kid that his or her mommy is a superhero and she's awesome.

I do that right in front of the employee because they could

be having the most kick-ass month and do amazing things all day long, but their family's never going to know about it. But if their boss is saying those things right in front of them? Oh man, it's huge!

When employees have their parents in town and bring them by the office, I run straight up to that person to give them the best handshake I can, look them right in the eyes, and say, "Thank you so much for giving birth to this amazing human being who's on my team. I cannot begin to tell you how valuable she is here. She's constantly doing amazing things to help us love people through finances, and it's beautiful. Thank you for raising this awesome person."

Intentionally affirm your employees in front of other people, and watch their faces light up. Watch their kids or spouse or parents puff up with pride. And you want to talk about creating fans of the business? Holy cow, people love hearing that their loved ones are amazing.

It took a lot of work and years of practicing to do this consistently, but now it's a trigger. If I see an employee with a family member anywhere at any time, I do my best to tell them a story of how awesome they are and affirm how important that employee is to our team. This practice brings joy to the employee's support system, makes a positive impact on the employee, and is one of the most fun things I get to do as a boss.

STEP SIX: AFFIRM BOTH POSITIVELY AND NEGATIVELY

So far, we've talked about how to affirm your team when you see them doing something right. But what happens when someone does something wrong? How do you course correct?

Most managers are probably wondering, "How do you keep people accountable? If I give them all this freedom, and I'm giving them high fives and affirmations, how do I keep them on track?"

If you have to let an employee know that they're doing the wrong thing, you'll still use affirmations—you'll just use negative affirmations. Contrary to popular belief, affirmations are not all gumdrops and rainbows and everybody getting a trophy. You do have to communicate negatively. Part of letting people know how they're doing is course correction.

Negative affirmations should be handled just like positive affirmations—they should be specific, and they should be given right away, on the spot if possible. People need to be affirmed as soon as possible—whether positively or negatively—in order to help them become masters of their craft. It's not reasonable to wait ninety days for a quarterly review to let your team know they're doing something wrong. That leaves the employee thinking,

"Wait, I've been doing this wrong for two months and you didn't say anything?"

You have to have the guts to communicate problems to your team right away. Not only does the employee appreciate it, but that gives you the opportunity to take an experience from potentially negative and turn it into a teaching moment. It's unbelievably effective to say, "You gave it a good effort, but here's how to approach it next time. Let's talk about it." Or, "Let's do it together." Or even, "Let's find a resource that can help."

The best way to negatively affirm people is to point everything to your unified purpose, which you will read about more in chapter 5.

The other day, I had to course correct one of my employees, so I just reminded her of the purpose we're all working toward: "Our goal is to love people, and we need to make sure they're being loved through finances. When you just did that, it was selfish, and being selfish is the antithesis of loving people well. You have to put the customer's needs before your own. I know you're tired, I know you've had a long day, but the best acts of love are when we can put other people's needs before our own."

People are more likely to change and be more accountable if you communicate how the course correction makes their life better and, more importantly, how it makes other people's lives better.

STEP SEVEN: BE EMOTIONALLY INTELLIGENT

It's easy to respond negatively when someone does something wrong, but it's important to control your emotions when giving course corrections.

There tend to be two types of managers: those who don't like confrontation and are afraid to affirm someone on the spot, and those who are reactionary and respond to missteps with hard-core reprimands. Neither of these approaches is effective when giving affirmations. If a manager is overly emotional when giving negative affirmations, the employees are only going to pick up on those emotions; they won't learn how to improve, which defeats the purpose of giving the course correction in the first place.

Anger is not something you want to use as a reflex, especially as a leader. I like to say that you should only be angry on purpose—and the only time I get angry on purpose is if someone intentionally hurts my team. For example, a couple of months ago, a vendor said something inappropriate to one of my team members. I called that vendor and let him—and everyone on my team—know how I angry I was about what had happened. Everyone could hear, see, and feel that anger. They probably don't remember the words I used, but they definitely remember the emotion.

With negative affirmations, on the other hand, you want your team to remember the *words*, not the emotion. You want to use the same tone of voice all the way through your explanation of what they did wrong that you don't want them to do again, to show that you have control. This improves how that correction will be received and ensures that the affirmation has a bigger impact.

STEP EIGHT: BE BALANCED

As you begin implementing both positive and negative affirmations, you'll want to make sure that you have a balance between the two.

Before giving an employee a negative affirmation in particular, look back to the last affirmation you gave them. Was it negative? If all you say is "You're doing it wrong," that beats up on people. Affirming is all about building confidence, so if you've given too many negative affirmations in a row, you may have to intentionally give a positive affirmation first.

If you have a hard time seeing the good, you're either not looking hard enough or not training them correctly. If you have a team member who consistently isn't doing what they're supposed to, they probably shouldn't be coming in the door every day.

Phil Jackson, one of the best coaches of all time and a spokesperson for the Positive Coaching Alliance, says that the magic ratio is five positive statements for every piece of constructive criticism.[21] Like him, you want to be the type of leader who is positively affirming more than negatively. Not only does this increase the chance of your team remembering all the great things they've done, it also allows them to redirect what they're doing while maintaining confidence.

STEP NINE: CELEBRATE!

Affirming is more than just words; you can celebrate and affirm your team with experiences.

How often do you celebrate?

We broke a record three months in a row, so we all went out for frozen yogurt across the street. The whole team ran down the stairs and across the street to the fro-yo place, making a ruckus as we all loaded up our ice cream with toppings.

---

21 https://devzone.positivecoach.org/resource/video/phil-jackson-magic-ratio

Once everyone was enjoying their treat, I said, "Guys, we're doing a lot of great things. We just broke another record. This is the number of people whose lives we've improved, and this is the financial impact our work has on their lives. You guys are awesome. Clink your frozen yogurt cups together like champagne glasses and let's celebrate with one another!"

It's just a simple statement and an inexpensive treat, but doing things like that creates an environment of celebrating with one another. Two months before, when we first broke the record, we went to a Brazilian steakhouse for all-you-can-eat meat-on-a-sword. The month before, we went to a movie theater with recliner chairs and servers who bring food and drink while you watch a movie.

Mixing up the way that you affirm people ensures that it's more sustainable and makes sure that the affirmations are better received.

REBUTTAL

"Grant," you may be thinking, "that sounds great and all, but I could never do that. I'm not that kind and happy-go-lucky. I don't manage people's emotions; that's not my job. I'm not here to give people fluff and be lovey-dovey. I run a business here, and in business we try to make money."

I want to remind you that statistically, affirmation provides confidence and confidence creates higher performing employees. When the pressure is on and you need them to perform, they're going to do better.

Yes, you run a for-profit business. Yes, profit is a big deal and money is important. Providing affirmation actually leads to making more money, because your team is operating at a higher level.

Affirmations are less about creating an environment of gumdrops and rainbows and more about leadership. People want to be led to a destination. Throughout that journey, they want to know if they're still headed in the right direction. Affirmations are a way to lead people through the maze. You may have to be stern at times—and we, as humans, need that additional guidance to steer us back on course after a misstep.

Or you may be thinking, "I don't know how to affirm my team. It's awkward to give positive notes on the spot because I'm not a good communicator."

That's okay. You're not alone. A lot of people struggle with coming up with things on the fly or communicating face-to-face. If you're not comfortable giving affirmations verbally, then put them in writing and give your employee a note. Or you can write down where they're doing a good job and read it to them. You don't even have to look them in the eye until you're more comfortable!

Start somewhere because little by little, you'll get better at it, too. Affirming people through clear communication is a skill you have to get good at, just like any other skill. The first time you make a sales call or write a blog post or create a video, it's usually terrible. But by the fiftieth time you do it, it gets better.

Externally, your rebuttal may be, "How can I ensure that everything is fair? How can I make sure that I'm affirming everybody equally?"

I've never had this issue in years of doing business. No one has ever come up to me and said, "Grant, you always say great things about this person, but you never say great things about that person."

If your heart is to affirm everyone, you can also affirm in teams. Sure, you're going to affirm individuals and let them know how they're doing, but you can celebrate as an entire team. Maybe you say, "Everyone on this team is doing great, and here's why and how it's making an impact."

Once affirming becomes a habit and you start doing it all the time, employees will notice—and they'll want to be noticed. They'll do the right thing and share it with their team so they can celebrate, too.

The best part is that affirming people is fun! Once you break through the awkwardness of not knowing how to do it because you've never done it before, it's a blast. It gives you so much joy as a boss and as a business owner. You can see that impact affirmations have on these individuals, how they walk around with a smile on their face and a bit more spring in their step.

FROM CONFIDENCE KILLER TO KILLER CONFIDENCE

I don't know anybody who thrives on only being told they're not doing a good job.

When Mike quit and I realized how much I was killing his confidence, I felt terrible. As I told you in the introduction, that's when I made a change and threw away those management books. I knew that I had to do better.

So when I hired a guy named Marshall, the former college sports coach I told you a bit about in chapter 1, I had my chance to be a better boss.

Marshall went from being a basketball coach to a position working behind a computer, setting up customer journeys, automations, and social media advertising. Way outside of his wheelhouse and not something he was technically skilled for. And when he first started, he was terrible. He had no idea what he was doing, and you could see on his face how much he was struggling.

At first, I had to work really hard to find something to affirm, but I told him every time he got something right. Sometimes I just affirmed him by saying, "Man, I was even worse at this! Let me tell you how badly I failed this one time..."

I continued providing information and education so Marshall could become a master of his craft. I affirmed him in front of the team, in front of his kids and wife. Little by little, he kept building, and I kept affirming until I was able to affirm him on really big stuff.

By the time he reached his one-year anniversary, he was better than I was when I used to do his job. He outthinks me, and he comes up with new ways of doing things to create better experiences for our customers, and he's thriving.

It gives me even more confidence to watch him kick butt because I know that if there's a problem with any of our automations, Marshall's going to be able to handle it—better than I could. He is a master of his craft, and he would not have become one without intentional affirmations.

Affirmation is more important than freedom. But if you can create a culture of freedom and affirmation—and then add a unified purpose, like you're going to see in chapter 4—you will create a culture of success and a company that wins.

KEY TAKEAWAYS

- Affirmations create confidence for your team, which is necessary for them to become masters of their craft.

- Negative affirmations are extremely important. They are used for course correction and to keep people accountable—but you should be positively affirming as much as, if not more than, you negatively affirm.

- People want to know how they are doing at work, so affirmations—whether positive or negative—should be given on the spot, not held until the next performance review.

MY INTENTIONAL ACTIONS

....

....

....

....

....

....

....

....

....

....

....

....

CHAPTER 4

PURPOSE CREATES IMPACT

I grew up in the church, and one of the things that really frustrated me was watching people be somebody at church on Sunday and then be a completely different person at their place of employment during the week.

They would put on a mask of piety when they were at church. But the mask came off and their true selves came out at work—and then their values such as integrity and ethics went out the window. Their mindset seemed to be, "Business is about profit, so we can do whatever the hell we want."

It bothered me to see that. There may be some slight nuances and adjustments for emotional intelligence reasons, but I think who you are, your ethos, should be the same in every scenario.

As I continued to discover what life is about and research the Bible, I wanted to simplify things and find purpose in my own life. So I wondered, "Who's the most important person in the Bible?" That's obvious—Jesus. So then let's simplify it further. What's the most important thing Jesus said? Maybe I can find something profound in those words.

I navigated to one of the last things He ever said. Makes sense that those words would be His most profound, right? I mean, if you knew you were going to die and leave the earth in the next fifteen minutes, you would probably choose your last words pretty carefully.

So toward the end of His life, after He died, rose from the grave, and He's about to ascend into heaven and leave the earth, Jesus said, "Go therefore and make disciples of all the nations, baptizing them in the name of the Father and the Son and the Holy Spirit."[22]

That's part of the Great Commission, which you've likely heard before because the church does a great job of sharing the importance of this statement.

But then I decided to break it down even more. What's the most important word in the most important statement made by the most important person? Go? Make? Baptiz-

_____
22   Matthew 28:19

ing? Those are action words, and they are very important, but they're not the *most* important. The most important word is the subject: them.

Whom do you "go" to? Them. Whom do you baptize? Them. Whom are you making disciples of? Them. This statement isn't even a complete thought without the word "them." Jesus made His entire life about serving and loving *them*.

That seemed to be a pretty decent example of what to make my life about. Even as I raise my children, I ask them, "What is life about?" *Others.* "What do we do with others?" *We love them.*

So what do I do in my business? Finances. What do I do in life? Love people. So my unified purpose is to love people through finances.

MAKE IT MATTER

I want to come back again to the statistic I'm sure you're familiar with by now: that nearly 88 percent of people aren't performing to their potential—but I want to focus on the 12 percent of people who *are*. What's different about those 12-percenters? They have a purpose.

As we established in chapter 1, more than 50 percent

of currently employed people are considering working somewhere else, primarily because they don't feel like the work they're doing has meaning.

When employees don't have a purpose, work feels mundane. They go through the motions but don't give it their all. They watch the clock instead of actively trying to solve problems and be in service. They become a liability more than an asset. They don't want to go to work, so they call in sick more. Their only reason for coming into work is to get money, so they try to manipulate the system to get as much money for as little work as possible. And without meaning to what they do, that is all those employees get—money.

People want to do work that matters—and you can give that to them.

When you create a purpose that makes coming to work every day worth it, you create a way to make the world a better place, one that makes a genuine impact on someone else's life for the positive.

The Ladders says that the number one thing top talent is looking for is a company that makes the world a better place or that provides a sense of meaning.[23]

---

23   https://www.theladders.com/career-advice/
       better-than-money-the-top-10-things-we-look-for-in-a-new-job

All of us, as a whole, want to make a positive impact on the people around us. A purpose is created when you can tie the service you provide or the product that you sell—as well as all the other tasks, activities, and things you do as part of your business—to a positive impact that's made on people.

At Stewardship, we provide home loans, insurance, and investments with wisdom and love. One aspect of what we do is giving people the biggest debt of their life, so how is that making a positive impact on them? Well, that debt provides many things for our customers. The obvious thing it provides is a home for them to live in, but with that comes a monthly expense—one that is likely the largest expense they have. But that large expense they have to pay helps them build equity in real property.

Psychologically, a home loan also leads to the fulfillment of the aspirational identity of becoming a homeowner. It gives the security of knowing they have a place to call *home*. Home is where they return after work, lay down their heads, dream, and make memories. The impact a mortgage makes on people is vast.

If you take the time to genuinely examine any product or service you provide, you can tie it to a positive impact on the end user or people in your community.

Most financial planners, mortgage companies, and insurance agencies set up their companies to make the most profit. We set up a company so that every piece of our structure is customer-centric. That's not just some statement; it's why I started a company: I wanted to make a positive impact on people, and finance is a big deal.

Let me be clear: my purpose is to love people through finances, but even though that purpose uses the word "love," I am not passionate about mortgages, insurance, or financial planning.

PASSION VERSUS PURPOSE

Purpose and passion are not the same thing. Most people are not passionate about mortgages. Passions are specific to a particular individual, and passions change.

I used to be passionate about my lawn, going to great lengths to make it green and beautiful. I would drive to specialty stores to find the perfect grass seed and just the right nitrogen pellets. I would even purchase cow manure and spread the fertilizer around with my hands! I mowed it on the weekends. I wanted it to look like the outfield at Wrigley, and I just loved having really great, green grass.

But a couple of weeks ago, as I was mowing my lawn, I thought, "I'm done. This takes so much time away from my family, and I don't want to do this anymore." My passion changed.

And again, passions are specific to an individual, so even if I were passionate about my grass, I wouldn't necessarily be able to unify a team around that.

A study done by UC Berkeley showed the difference between passion and purpose at work. They found that people who had a purpose, who found meaning in their work, outperformed the people who had passion.[24]

This isn't just true at work, though; it's been shown throughout history.

Freud was all about passion. He basically said that people exist and do whatever they want to do because of passion. Viktor Frankl, however, showed that the opposite is true. Frankl not only proved this through countless studies as a neurologist and psychiatrist, he personally demonstrated it in one of the most trying experiences anyone could ever go through. You see, Frankl survived Theresienstadt, Kaufering, Türkheim, and Auschwitz concentration camps during the Holocaust—and he was instrumental in helping a large group of other people to survive as well.

---

24 https://peopleacuity.com/which-is-more-important-passion-or-purpose/

In an unimaginable situation that required extreme motivation to continue living, Frankl had to help people find purpose. There was no passion in the concentration camps. Had those people been dependent on passion to see them through, they all would have died. But Frankl gave them the purpose of staying alive so they could tell the world the truth about the horrors the Nazis were perpetrating. That purpose—intended to help the rest of the world come together to prevent these atrocities from ever happening again—kept him and many other people alive.

Later, in his behavioral science research, Frankl found that people who pursue passion are unable to find purpose. The pursuit of passion is a negative impact of not being able to find purpose—but a leader can give those people purpose.

As a leader, you and your company culture can focus on a purpose that is about others. When executed well, a purpose requires sacrifice. It requires putting others' needs ahead of your own. And it requires trying to make an impact on other people. It requires selflessness.

I have an amazing team, and I don't have one person who's passionate about mortgages. But they love people, and they will stop at nothing to ensure that those people are loved through finances.

HOW TO CREATE YOUR UNIFIED PURPOSE

At this point, you may be wondering what your unified purpose is. Is it your mission statement? Vision statement? Core values?

Not really.

Remember, this book is about your *internal* company culture. That means your team and your employees—and you. Your unified purpose comes from you and is used to motivate your team; it's not an advertising slogan meant to motivate the public to choose your product or service.

But don't worry. As foreign as this may sound, my four-step process will help you create the purpose around which you will unify your team.

STEP ONE: IDENTIFY THE PROBLEMS YOUR CUSTOMER HAS

Creating your unified purpose starts by identifying what problems your customer has.

According to Donald Miller, founder of Story Brand and author of *Building a StoryBrand*, customers have three different types of problems: external, internal, and philosophical.

An external problem is the one we can see. For us in finance, the external problem our clients have is that they need a home loan so they can buy a house. They need car insurance so they can drive a car. Or they need their investments managed wisely so they can accomplish their goals. These are all external problems, and they are fairly easily identified.

An internal problem is how a customer feels about their external problem. We may not see it, and they might not even say it out loud, but they are thinking about that problem. Even more, they *feel* something about it.

Our customers, for example, may feel uncertain about their financial future. They may have a growing salary or retirement account but no idea how it will help them meet their goals or live their preferred lifestyle. They dream about retiring, but they don't know when they'll be able to do it—or if this dream is even realistic. More importantly, they aren't sure what steps to take between now and then, to make sure their retirement dreams come true.

This uncertainty creates fear and insecurities. They don't have confidence, they don't know if they can do it, and they may feel inadequate. Recognizing the internal problem means identifying those feelings the customer has.

The philosophical problem is even more important than

both the external and internal problems. To discover the philosophical problem, you want to ask, "Why is it *just plain wrong* that people are dealing with these external and internal problems?"

This is different from the external problem. It shouldn't look like, "They need insurance so they can drive a car," or "They need their money managed for retirement." You want something stronger than that. Looking to your customers' internal problem, considering what they're thinking and feeling, can help, but the best way to create a strong, unified purpose is to identify the problem as a philosophical issue. Why is this wrong as a society? Why is it wrong that people are dealing with this? Why would a large number of people *care* that this is wrong?

We recognize that homeownership is a really big deal, not just to your finances but also to consistency and cohesiveness in your family. And at Stewardship, we think it's just plain wrong that people don't know that they can do it. Remember our purpose, "Loving people through finances"? The philosophical problem our customers are experiencing is that they don't get loved in financial situations.

Most personal financial salespeople will try to take advantage of them. They will look right in someone's eyes and figure out, "How much money can I make off this person?"

They'll sell products or services that may not be the best solution for the customer—but it pays the advisor the most commission.

This is especially true in the world of investment management. Most financial professionals sell a stock or mutual fund to a customer because it will pay them a big commission, not because it's 100 percent best for the customer. Sales reps for these mutual funds come into brokerage offices to tout their wares. As they work to convince the financial professionals to sell their investments to their customers, they may talk a little about performance, but it's mostly about the commission the fund pays to the financial advisors and the incentives and trips they will qualify for if they sell it to their customer base.

We don't do that at Stewardship because, when it comes to your personal finances, we believe that is especially wrong. Why? Because it dramatically impacts your life! It impacts your goals and your finances on a day-to-day, month-to-month, and year-to-year basis, and those finances impact your relationships.

Having money problems will make you work more. If a financial professional sells you an investment that is not 100 percent best for you, then it can give you money problems. That financial professional is stealing time—time that you now have to commit to working more to pay off that extra debt, potentially delaying retirement or other financial goals. That additional work is time away from your family—all so the investment advisor can get more commission and qualify for a trip to Puerto Rico.

Time is the most precious resource on the planet, so it's *just plain wrong* that many finance companies will put you in a bad spot for their own good.

The philosophical problem is a *big* problem, one that creates emotion. When people get charged up and that problem is solved, it creates a sense of belonging. It creates a high level of happiness and joy. And ideally, it even creates an aspirational identity. People believe they are a certain type of person because they are fighting this injustice, or they believe they're a better person for solving this philosophical issue.

You can unify a lot of people around finding a solution for a philosophical problem, and this is where you can create a movement.

Take some time right now to figure out the problems your clients or customers are dealing with. Start by writing down the external problems; these are easy. You see them and solve them every day for your customers.

Now go a level deeper. What negative feelings do those

external problems cause for your customer? Write those down.

Then go deeper still. Why is it *just plain wrong* that people have to deal with that? How do those problems make our society and our world worse?

STEP TWO: ANSWER "WHAT DO YOU DO?"

With that philosophical problem identified, you can move on to answering the question, "What do you do?" What is it that your company actually does?

At Stewardship, we write home loans, we write insurance policies, we manage investments, we offer money management. But we don't want to identify all of that, so we just say, "We help people with money."

In your answer to what you do, you want to use an emotionally charged word that connects people with the philosophical problem you established in step one.

Let's look at some other companies' unified purposes so you can see what I mean:

- Airbnb: To create a world where everyone belongs
- Kellogg's: Nourishing families so they can flourish and thrive

- Disney: To use our imagination to bring happiness to millions
- Southwest Airlines: To give people the freedom to fly
- Stewardship: Love people through finances

So if we look at that list, what does Airbnb do? They rent out vacation homes online. They give people a place to stay. But their unified purpose is to create a world where everyone belongs. So what do they do? They create belonging. That's emotionally charged and it's *just plain wrong* if people don't belong.

What does Kellogg's do? They make cereal. Their unified purpose is nourishing families so they can flourish and thrive. Who doesn't think families should be nourished? It's *just plain wrong* if they're not.

Southwest Airlines gives people the freedom to fly. The emotionally charged word there is "freedom." Who doesn't want freedom? Who hasn't dreamed about flying?

If we look just at the "what do you do?" answers, Airbnb creates a world. Kellogg's nourishes. Disney uses imagination. Southwest gives. What do we do at Stewardship? We love. The philosophical problem we've identified is that people get taken advantage of, they aren't loved through finances. So what are we going to do? We're going to love.

What is it that you do—and which emotionally charged word, like "belonging," "freedom," "nourish," or "love," can you include in that answer?

STEP THREE: IDENTIFY WHOM YOU SERVE

The third step in creating your unified purpose is to identify whom you serve.

You're not looking to identify a demographic, such as thirty-five-year-old males who live in the suburbs. You're looking for a word that people can connect with, one that they identify with. If my unified purpose was "loving females through finances," all the males on my staff would have a hard time connecting with that purpose.

What are the words people connect with in our other examples? Who is served by each company? For Airbnb, it's "the world." You're in the world, and you probably think the world should be a better place—so it connects. For Kellogg's, it's "families." You probably either have a family or have been part of a family.

The word can be as simple as "people," like in Southwest's purpose. You're a person. I'm a person. We're all people—and so we can all be served by Southwest (and Stewardship, for that matter!). Disney just says "millions," but you can be part of those millions—if you want happiness. And who doesn't want happiness?

As you identify whom you serve, you want to find that word that people connect with. Is it "everyone"? Is it "family"? Maybe it's "society" or "millions of people." It can even be your town or state. Whatever the word is, you want it to be something people will be able to identify with, especially the people on your staff.

STEP FOUR: ANSWER "WHAT IS THE OUTCOME?"

The final step in creating your unified purpose is to answer, "What is the outcome?" The outcome is the opposite of the philosophical problem you identified in step one. Remember, that problem makes the world crappy—your outcome needs to be something that makes the world better.

Airbnb makes people feel like they belong, so the outcome is belonging. For Kellogg's, the outcome is flourishing and thriving. Disney's outcome is the same as what they do, and that's happiness. What's the outcome for Southwest? Well, when you get to fly, you get freedom. With Stewardship, what we do is the same as the outcome: we love.

But so far, you just have a collection of parts, just a bunch of words. To actually form the unified purpose, you just put steps one through four together.

Take the action word of what you do, the noun of whom you serve, and the preferred outcome or happy ending. Put all of those together, and you have your unified purpose.

Let me break it down for you, using the Stewardship example:

- Action of what we do: love through finances
- Noun of whom we serve: people
- Happy ending: being loved
- Put it together: We love people through finances

Pretty simple when you look at it that way, right? I know you can do it!

AM I DOING IT RIGHT?

I have a checklist for you to go through as you create your unified purpose. Ask yourself the following questions to determine if you're on the right track:

IS IT SIMPLE?

Your unified purpose needs to be extremely simple, because it needs to be repeatable. If it's a long sentence that you can't remember or say in one breath, that's not a good idea because ultimately you are going to point everything toward this unified purpose. Keeping it simple makes it easier to connect with. "Love people through finances" is four words. The fewer words, the better. It doesn't even have to be a complete sentence; it can be a simple phrase.

When I first tried this, I created a mission statement and a vision statement and core values, just like they say to do in business school. I looked up the definition of a steward: "a person who manages another's property or financial affairs with providence and moral excellence."

I thought that sounded sophisticated because it had long words, so I created, "Stewardship exists to enrich the lives of Arizona residents by managing their real estate finances with providence and moral excellence."

Simple? No. Easy to say? Absolutely not. And worst of all, that sounds nothing like me.

As you come up with your unified purpose, don't overcomplicate it. Don't worry about using thirty-dollar words. Keeping it simple will make sure it is easy to understand so that when your team is unified around your purpose, it's clear just what that purpose is.

DOES IT MAKE THE WORLD A BETTER PLACE?

Your purpose needs to make the world a better place. It has to make an impact on other people. It's got to be meaningful and helpful, and it needs to specifically solve the philosophical problem that is making the world a worse place.

This is extremely important because solving a philosophical problem is what makes your purpose unifying. Every healthy person wants to help others. We all have a desire to make the world a better place. When your unified purpose accomplishes that, it becomes a rallying cry!

DOES IT REQUIRE SACRIFICE, SELFLESSNESS, OR SERVING?

The best way to determine if your unified purpose is going to make the world a better place is to ask if it requires sacrifice, selflessness, or serving. If you are going to show up every day in the office and sacrifice your time, energy, and effort to do this thing, it means that you are fundamentally acting in selflessness. You cannot sacrifice without selflessness. And if there's selflessness, you're focusing on serving others, which means you're making an impact on other people.

Loving people through finances means that we have to put others' needs ahead of our own. If we don't, it's not very loving.

DOES IT CREATE A CONNECTION WITH YOUR TEAM?

Your purpose needs to unify your team. Typically, if it requires that sacrifice, it will unify them. If they are part of or at least care about the people you serve, that will also help unify your team around your purpose.

DOES IT CONTAIN AN EMOTIONALLY CHARGED WORD?

We talked about this in step three, but your unified purpose should contain an emotionally charged word. For me, it's the word "love." As it pertains to the finance industry, that's a super-weird word to use—and it stands out. It stays with people, creates curiosity, and makes them wonder about our company.

One of my Culture Course students is the owner of an insurance company. His first stab at creating his unified purpose was, "My unified purpose is to make an impact on people through insurance."

Okay, cool. But what do you really care about? How do you want to make an impact on people? How are you going to make an impact on people that solves this philosophical problem? What are people dealing with that is *just plain wrong*?

He replied, "I can't stand it when people are apathetic. I think people should be inspired."

"There you go!" I affirmed him. "Inspiring is a big, emotionally charged word."

So he changed it to, "Making an inspiring impact on people through insurance."

"Great job," I said, "but can you make it even simpler?"

His unified purpose turned out to be, "Inspiring people through insurance." I'm a person. I like being inspired. Perfect.

All he did was change one word and simplify the statement, but by looking at what he gets charged up about, an issue that makes him emotional, he nailed it.

IS IT *YOU*?

This is the most important question to ask. Your unified purpose isn't just about coming up with words and putting them together. If you don't really care about it, if it's not really you as a business owner and leader, people are going to feel that inauthenticity. They'll know if you're faking it. Pointing everything toward something you don't really care about is not going to work.

It is vital to connect the unified purpose of your business with *your* personal purpose. It can't be separated; the purpose has to be *you*.

Remember the frustration I felt as I struggled to find my personal purpose, which I told you about at the beginning of this chapter? That frustration stemmed from seeing people act one way at certain times and completely different at others. You can't have a purpose full of integrity at home but then create a purpose for your business that is based on making as much money as possible if it means taking advantage of people.

I found the unified purpose I use in my business by first understanding my *life's* purpose. If we swap out the word "love" for "health" in my purpose, it could become "Making people's finances healthy." That's fine, but it doesn't have meaning for *me*—but loving people does.

If you are struggling with this part of your unified purpose, ask yourself a few questions: Does your purpose feel authentic, or does it feel like you're pretending to be someone else? Say it out loud. Does it sound like you? Does it evoke emotion in you? Is it something you genuinely care about? Read it in front of the mirror, then think back over your life. What are you living for? Does your purpose somehow connect to that? Does fulfilling this unified purpose with your company somehow also help you fulfill your life's purpose?

Another one of my Culture Course students was having a hard time with his unified purpose. He couldn't find an emotionally charged word, and he was struggling to make it *him*.

He also runs an insurance agency, but when we chatted in the Culture Course Facebook group about what he *really* likes to do, it's basketball. He loves coaching it, he loves being in the gym, and he loves hearing the squeak of sneakers on the gym floor. Listening to him talk, I realized that I could relate. I play basketball, too, so I could put myself in his shoes. "It sounds like what you love about basketball is competing."

"That's it, man!" he said. "I love to compete."

"So why don't you use that word? The word 'compete' is emotionally charged, and it's *you*."

The unified purpose he created for his insurance agency is "Competing for clients' protection." That stands out. That's a purpose he can talk to his team about. If he notices they're not doing something correctly, he can ask them, "Did you compete right there? Did you give everything you had?" When they do something well, he can say, "That's how we compete! Good job."

TROUBLESHOOTING

Another Culture Course student absolutely nailed his unified purpose. He gets really irritated when people waste his time because he recognizes that time is a valuable resource. Every minute of his time that is wasted is one less minute he gets with his wife and kids.

He also sells insurance, but he wanted to make insurance simple for people. He thought it was annoying that people have to call in and deal with call centers. It's a waste of time. So he created systems to make buying insurance easier. He'll stop at nothing to make sure that the people his business serves don't have their time wasted. His unified purpose is "Giving the gift of time through simple insurance solutions." How great is that?

He is, quite literally, giving people the gift of time through his extremely efficient systems and intelligently designed, simple process. Whenever he talks to his team, he can say, "Are we saving time today?" When somebody helps a client save time, he says, "That means this person is going to have time today they didn't have yesterday. They might be able to play catch with their kid or have an extra moment with their wife that otherwise would have been stolen from them. Well done!"

Don't try to be somebody you're not. You don't have to be a poet or a wordsmith if that's not you. Don't just use words that sound good if you don't use them in your life or if it's not something that you really care about.

You should be able to tell a story about your purpose. When I say, "We love people through finances," the reason we do is because if we don't, they're going to get their finances handled somewhere else, and those people might take advantage of them. And that means that people in our society may get hurt financially. When people are hurt financially, their relationships are hurt, too.

That story leads to making an impact on people.

It should be something you can say with pride, no matter who asks you or where you are when they ask. The best way to do that is to make obvious the impact you make on other people. Your purpose shouldn't be, "We do insurance to make as much money as possible." Instead, it's more, "We help others and put them in a better place."

If you want to look at it from another angle, we can use another tip from Donald Miller. In one of his Business

Made Simple videos, he said, "If you want to rally your team around people, fill in this blank: We save people from_____."

It's okay to tap into something you really dislike, something that pisses you off, something that creates emotion within you. Don't be scared to take your heart and mind there. We save people from getting screwed on their finances.

If you put yours together and it feels boring or "meh," go back to that emotion. What do you like? What do you really dislike? What gets you riled? Tell me a story of the last time you were really pissed off or really emotionally high. How'd you get to that place? Let's find the word or words that are attached to that feeling.

If you put your unified purpose together and think that it's boring, guess what? You're like 99 percent of people who put theirs together the first time. Almost no one gets it right the first time—and that's okay.

What you just wrote down is a place to start. And at least you *are* starting. A lot of people aren't even thinking about this. Just the fact that you're reading this book, putting together a purpose that will unify your team, is better than almost everybody else.

Keep going. Don't give up. Make adjustments if you need

to. Think through it; talk to other people. When you put it together, you'll know. You've got this!

Don't get discouraged.

Your unified purpose is not carved in stone. You can change it. You created this, and it can and should be adjusted. You don't have to get it exactly right the first time.

But when you get fired up about it—and you know you can get other people fired up—you're on the right track.

The ultimate check is to ask yourself if you can keep your team accountable with this unified purpose. Can you affirm your team with it? Can you ask, "Was that inspiring? Was that loving? Was that competing? Was that saving people time?"

That doesn't mean that you create this with your team. Your unified purpose won't be created by committee. It has to come from you as the leader. You're the one who unifies people around this purpose. You're going to lead by example. So you have to figure out what gets you fired up. Why did you start your business? Why have you not sold your business yet? What makes you continue to pursue it? Yes, you make money, but there's something about it that makes an impact and makes the world a better place. You have to dig deep and try to find that.

REBUTTAL

Internally, you might say to yourself, "Grant, this won't work because you don't understand my business. We don't really do things that make an impact. We're way too B2B."

To find out whom your company impacts, you just have to continue down the line of end users. Whom does your business serve—and then whom does *that* business serve? Who is the end user, and what does their life look like? Or what are the lives like of the employees in the businesses you serve?

For us, we're loving people through finances, but what does that mean to an investment portfolio? We're getting people this investment, but I have to continue to go down the line to the individual level, focusing on telling the story of how this investment makes an impact on that one person.

We get them the investment by listening to their actual needs, which means it's going to meet their goals. They have a goal to stop working by a certain date, or to pay for their kid's college, or to make their money stretch as far as possible. We help them do that so they can be less stressed about money. When they're less stressed, they have more energy to focus on things that matter like their relationships with their spouse and kid.

The client has a purpose of being able to better provide for their family, and they feel like they're doing a great job because their money is working for them, because we listen to the client's needs and put them in an investment portfolio that aligns with their goals, and their heart, and their integrity.

More importantly, our ideal client *wants* to spend their time focusing on their family, not stressing about their financial future. They are confident that Stewardship is handling their finances so they can have a better quality of life. They don't have to spend the mental energy managing their money or worrying about the future; instead, they can make the most of the moments they have. They trust in us because they know their finances are being handled with wisdom and love. As a result, we're creating a world that our client actually cares about.

Sometimes, to find the impact of your purpose, you just have to continue to go deeper, step by step by step. Eventually, what you do impacts somebody somewhere.

Even if that fails and you can't find anybody who is directly impacted by your company, you can make an impact with the profits from your business. You can be part of philanthropic endeavors as your purpose. Look at TOMS Shoes. Their purpose is to take the profit from people buying their shoes and then give shoes away to people who need them. So there's more than one way that purpose can make an impact.

Or you might be thinking, "This is too fluffy. This is not me. I'm a business guy. I'm not here to provide purpose for people. They can go find meaning elsewhere. My purpose is to give them a paycheck."

Well, that's not what science tells us. Countless studies prove that that attitude perpetuates the problem we have in this society. Look at yourself in the mirror. How do you genuinely feel, being money motivated? What was the real reason you got into this business? At some point, as the owner of the business, you were enchanted with the impact being made—even if that impact was to get money to grow opportunities for your family.

If you don't give your team purpose intentionally, they're going to go find it somewhere else. But when you do provide purpose, your team is going to take such pride in what they do and where they work, they're not just going to tell customers but also their friends and family and their community. Then you're going to have a new problem: everyone is going to want to come work for you!

Implementing your unified purpose may seem like this big, hairy, audacious thing, but it starts with something simple, and that is you living out that purpose with your team. We'll look at how to unify your team around that purpose and point everything you do toward it in the next chapter.

KEY TAKEAWAYS

- A unified purpose creates the most impact because it genuinely helps people by solving an external, internal, and philosophical problem for them.

- Your company's unified purpose must first connect to your life's purpose. What matters most to you? How can you use that emotion in the purpose for your business, to solve problems and create the biggest impact for other people?

- Purpose brings people together. This purpose will guide you and your team to solve the problems you encounter. With a purpose, people will love being a part of your team, too. Together, you will make a real difference.

MY INTENTIONAL ACTIONS

CHAPTER 5

POINT EVERYTHING TOWARD YOUR UNIFIED PURPOSE

In 2007, when I was twenty-five years old, I started my first business, Stewardship Mortgage. From the beginning, I planned to add all of the financial services we now have: mortgages, insurance, financial planning, investment management—with even more to come.

I had seen other people in the mortgage industry rip off clients, giving them terrible mortgages just to earn a few extra dollars in commission for their next BMW purchase. Families were hurt because of these mortgages. The bad mortgage led to money fights with their spouse, which then led to those customers getting a divorce. As I watched family after family fall apart due to financial issues, all I could think was, *"This is not how business should be done."*

Our mission at Stewardship—the heart of everything we do—is to love people through finances. Whether they know it or not, our clients are going to get the best deal possible. We make sure, as much as we possibly can, that the finances we steward aren't going to lead to a divorce, or become a cause of frustration with their children, or even impact their relationship with God. We don't want finances to hinder people's lives; we want their lives to be enhanced.

And I've only been able to achieve these goals because of my amazing team. This is not a trite statement that leaders are supposed to say with humility. My business literally could not accomplish everything we have accomplished—and everything we continue to achieve—without the incredible, selfless employees who give their all, day in and day out.

My small team of just over twenty people consists of top producers, all of whom are nationally ranked and have won numerous awards, including Top 1 Percent and Top 100 in the country.

My employees are better at closing mortgages than I ever was. They break records constantly. One employee was able to accomplish in one month more than two times the amount most people do in a *year*—or even two! And that high performance is not exclusive to just this one employee. As I'm writing this book, another employee is about to break the aforementioned employee's record—which had been set only a couple of weeks before. We don't have just one standout employee; we have an entire team of thriving superstars.

These are awards that I never came close to obtaining on my own. I was pretty good at my job when I met with customers and handled transactions, but all of my employees have broken my records and are far exceeding the production amounts I was ever capable of on my own.

They are able to do this because they care about people. Everyone genuinely cares about what we're doing here at Stewardship. My team knows that the records they're breaking aren't just production numbers. Those transactions are attached to people. They're transactions that make a positive impact on people, households, families, quite literally giving them better insurance, home loans, and investments as a result of working with us.

The team knows that the people we serve are receiving exactly what they should—finances handled with wisdom and love.

PURSUING PURPOSE TOGETHER

In a *Psychology Today* article titled "The Power of Purpose," Steve Taylor writes, "The need for purpose is one of the defining characteristics of human beings. Human beings crave purpose, and we suffer serious difficulties when we do not have it."[25]

We can bring that need for purpose into the workplace as well. You can show your team that they don't have to spend a big part of their lives at work and then go find purpose outside the office. Instead, they can find purpose through the work they do. Not only that, but your purpose can actually unify your team and bring them together.

Pat McMillan, who is a big leader of teams doing amazing things such as climbing Mount Everest, says that a clear and compelling purpose is important to individual team members and, in fact, "is the single biggest factor in team success."[26]

A unified purpose is one that can be done with other people and for other people. It's a purpose you aren't bashful or embarrassed to share but one that you are proud of. A unified purpose creates a connection with a community and makes the world a better place.

---

25   https://www.psychologytoday.com/us/blog/out-the-darkness/201307/the-power-purpose

26   Pat MacMillan, *The Performance Factor* (Nashville: B&H Publishing Group, 2001), 44.

Without unifying your team around a purpose, it just feels like a collection of individuals doing their own thing. If everybody's going in different directions, how are you supposed to lead?

But with everybody working together toward that unified purpose, you're all going to be able to do a lot more and make a bigger impact. When everybody is on the same team and the same mission, the individuals on that team are going to grow more. If one person has a bad day, the others can help pick them up. They can help one another grow and hold one another accountable.

My staff calls one another family. They hang out with one another because they genuinely want to, because they care about one another. And that helps them enjoy coming to work, too. We all come together to love people through finances. And the social engagement and relational connection of my team is on a completely different level than in most companies.

Ultimately, unification does two things. First, it simplifies your life as a business owner, as a manager, and as the leader of your team. Second, it increases performance— and that makes your life easier, too!

When people are unified around a shared purpose, they perform at a higher level. There's a higher sense of social engagement. They feel more happiness and joy, which stimulates feel-good receptors in their brains and enables them to perform better.

A unified purpose also creates a healthy sense of social pressure. If someone knows they're not performing as well as they could be, they're not going to think, "Oh man, I've got to do this thing or my boss is going to get mad at me." Instead, they think, "I've got to do this thing because if I don't, it's going to affect my coworker—whom I care about, who's my friend—and their life isn't going to be as good."

This is a big deal! Because of the social pressure created around a unified purpose, there is also a social responsibility. My team *wants* to complete their tasks and do a great job—without my having to spend a lot of time and energy keeping them accountable. They keep one another on track, and that accountability is more effective than my telling them what to do.

One of my employees was going to be out of the office for some time because her husband was having knee surgery. The rest of the team, instead of worrying about how her absence would affect them, came together and asked, "How can we help?"

I didn't have to tell them to step up or give orders. I didn't have to implement any policies or procedures. They just did it because they care about one another—and about our clients. They care about our unified purpose of loving people through finances. That is always the goal, no matter how it's achieved.

At the end of the day, we all want employees who care, and a unified purpose makes it so your team cares about one another, about the company, and about your mission.

Combining freedom and affirmation with a unified purpose is the key to having a self-managed team. With these three motivators in place, you can put yourself in the CEO position. You can have people who are not task-completion specialists but who are part of a team that works together to fulfill your vision with a sense of responsibility—and without your having to micromanage every step. Then you, as CEO, can come to the team with ideas and endeavors to move the business forward and make a bigger impact. You can build a business as the visionary and ambassador of your brand.

HOW TO POINT EVERYTHING TOWARD YOUR PURPOSE

The human resources company ERC defines culture as "the character and personality of your organization. It's what makes your organization unique and is the sum of its values, traditions, beliefs, interactions, behaviors, and attitudes."[27]

The personality of your organization is going to be shaped based on the reason your team comes into work: their purpose. What makes your organization unique? Its purpose. The sum of its values, traditions, and beliefs are exactly your unified purpose.

Having a unified purpose and making an impact on people sounds cool, but how do you actually point everything toward that purpose?

IT STARTS WITH YOU

Harvard Business Review, Forbes, Inc., Warwick, and other journals have done numerous studies that show that employees produce at higher levels if they believe their supervisor or boss is someone who cares about them as a person.

If you are a leader pursuing a unified purpose that makes an impact on people and makes the world a better place, you need to make an impact first on each employee as an individual. You need to help every member of your team see that this place of employment, your business,

---

27 https://www.yourerc.com/blog/post/
    workplace-culture-what-it-is-why-it-matters-how-to-define-it

is about making a positive impact on others—including the positive impact you're seeking to make on your employees. Then you and your entire team can pursue your unified purpose as well as the mission of making the world a better place—because their world is a great place and you make it a little better.

UNIFY YOUR TEAM THROUGH FREEDOM AND AFFIRMATION

Unifying your team around the purpose that you created in the previous chapter starts with the freedom and affirmation we talked about in chapters 2 and 3.

Freedom and affirmation must point toward your unified purpose. What does that mean? You only give the types of freedom and affirmation that are in sync with your unified purpose.

I don't care how much my staff is on their phones, playing video games, taking breaks, or going on vacation—as long as they are loving people through finances. As the leader, you can see, "If I give them this freedom, it helps them pursue the unified purpose better."

To selflessly and genuinely serve people, you have to sacrifice—a lot. It can wear on you—and your team. Our team serves people, which means we have to be ready to talk to people at almost every hour of the day, every day of the week. Our advisors answer phone calls, emails, and text messages, engaging in conversations with customers, even on nights and weekends sometimes. Why? Because that's the best way to serve the customer.

I give my team freedom to manage their workday because I know that there are rare occasions when they're answering their phones at nine o'clock on Saturday night when a client calls them. Why do I do that? Because that's the best way to serve my team, who is serving our clients, pursuing our unified purpose, and making a difference in our community. Giving them this freedom helps them serve selflessly.

I give that extra amount of freedom so they can love people better.

To give your team the freedom they need, you have to understand your own unified purpose and how it will be met. If you run a retail store or coffee shop, you can't really let your team come and go as they please. But because you know what your unified purpose is, that gives you a baseline to draw from and determine the types of freedom you are able to give.

If you do run a coffee shop, for example, perhaps you give your employees the freedom to take breaks whenever they want. "But, Grant," you may be asking, "what if they take a break when customers are coming in the door?"

Well, that wouldn't be pursuing the unified purpose, which, for a coffee shop, likely has something to do with serving people. So if people need to be served in that moment, you don't take a break then. But when there are moments people don't need to be served, your employees can have some time to themselves. The freedom and unified purpose work together to give your team the self-management to be able to act without taking cues from you.

Finally, every time you affirm your team, every time you celebrate with them, point it toward your unified purpose. I often find myself saying, "Let's celebrate together because we loved people through finances. We made a huge impact on people." It's not about, "Hey, let's celebrate because we hit this number." It's always celebrating that we are living out our unified purpose.

This not only allows you to connect accomplishments and affirmation to work that matters on a big level, it also allows you to celebrate and affirm the smaller things, too. I might say, for example, "You guys! Every single one of our reviews has been responded to by someone on our team. That means that each one of those people knows that their review has been seen and heard. *That is loving.* Well done!"

When you give affirmation and freedom in line with a unified purpose, it creates an environment of infectious success. People are winning here. People see that you are having amazing success—and they want to do that, too. Movement is attractive. We are attracted to movement, but sometimes it feels like we get stuck doing the same tasks over and over again with no end or purpose in sight. You can create positive movement. You can create something attractive for your team when you affirm with your unified purpose in mind.

Your team wants to come to the office every day because they are excited about the success they are going to achieve today. And when you do it really well, people in your community will see the movement and be attracted to it, too. This is where the tide turns. Instead of having to go look for new employees, they come to you! They want to be part of a team that is unified—and winning.

MAKE SURE EVERYONE ALIGNS WITH YOUR PURPOSE

Having a unified purpose makes the tough decisions you have to make as a business owner easier.

Someone who doesn't fit in isn't a bad person, but they are most likely a bad fit to the culture of your team. If everyone else is pursuing your unified purpose—and pursuing it well—the person who's a poor fit will stick out like a sore thumb. The decision of whether or not to let them go will basically be made for you, because it will be obvious not only to you but to everyone else—including that employee.

When you have to let somebody go, it typically has a huge negative impact on your company's culture. Everyone else wonders, "Am I going to get fired, too?" Then they start coming to the office and doing their job with fear, and as we discussed in chapter 3, fear creates hesitation, not the confidence and positivity you want people acting in to be able to perform better.

But when you let somebody go because they're not a good culture fit, your whole team will see that it was the right thing to do. Again, it will be obvious when someone on the team is not working with everyone else to pursue the purpose. That lack of unity is easy to see. Instead of being fearful or frustrated, the rest of your team will be able to pursue your unified purpose even better.

If your employees can identify with your unified purpose— which is selfless, which requires sacrifice, which is about making an impact on other people—then you want them on your team. If not, you don't. It's that simple.

NO, SERIOUSLY, POINT *EVERYTHING* TOWARD YOUR PURPOSE

Every single task that you do is now attached to your unified purpose. At Stewardship, we can test every task by saying, "We do this because it leads to that, which then allows people to be loved." In that way, every single member of your team feels the importance of each task they complete and how it makes an impact on others.

You're going to hire differently. When you create a job posting, instead of saying, "We're hiring for this position, and here's how much it pays," you can say, "We're adding to our family and we need more people to love people through finances. If you're good at loving others and you want to make a big impact on our community, submit your résumé."

A lot of people make the mistake of hiring the person who is the most skilled or has the best résumé. The top talent in the world isn't somebody who has a really cool certificate or a certain amount of experience; the top talent are the people who are self-motivated, who can work hard, who are humble and willing to grow. Do not hire someone based on a résumé. Don't choose someone because of the skills they list. Hire to attributes and character first. That will help make sure they are aligned with the unified purpose, ensuring a perfect fit.

As you go through the hiring process, you're going to determine, "Is this person aligned with my purpose? Can I trust them to pursue this unified purpose with everything they've got?"

Taking these steps will not only make it easier to find the best fit, it'll save you a lot of money, too. A unified purpose dramatically increases retention, and retention is an unbelievable way to increase profit on your P & L statement because it lowers expenses for rehiring. Retention also allows people to continue to get better at something, which means they're more productive. And the more they produce, the more profit you'll have, too.

You're going to manage differently. You're going to take all of those mundane tasks that people get burned out on and have no meaning or purpose behind them, and you're going to give them meaning. Make them important. Show how those tasks make a real impact on people. Create a story that connects the sacrifice your employees make to the unified purpose being met.

You're going to train differently. Your meetings are going to have your unified purpose as part of them. Your continuing education. Your handbook. It's all going to have that unified purpose woven into it. That's how you are going to serve your team—by giving them the why behind all the things they're learning and doing.

The other way you can serve your team while pursuing your unified purpose together is by encouraging each employee to be the best version of themselves—and giving them freedom to do so.

We can all do only so much in a day, which means that we must be good stewards of the things we ask of our staff. We are physically limited—and each of us has different limits. We have only so much energy we can put into a particular day or week. If we have to act differently than we would normally—if we have to put on a mask to go to work, using a voice we don't typically use or wearing clothes we don't typically wear—it makes it much harder to consistently perform at a high level. Asking your employees to do something outside of what is natural for them is also asking them to use their precious energy and effort for something other than serving your clients.

If you need people to talk and act a certain way, hire those people who are comfortable talking and acting that way, and then give them the freedom to be in that. Ask yourself what might prevent your team from being themselves. Are those things necessary, or could that energy be better used somewhere else?

Being selfless and sacrificing takes a certain amount of energy. I don't want my employees wasting energy putting on a mask or an uncomfortable wardrobe and being somebody they're not or acting differently around me or their coworkers; I want them using all of that energy on serving our clients. I want them pursuing our unified purpose, because that takes selflessness. It takes sacrifice. It takes hard work. I want them to have that energy to spend on loving people through finances, because that is what matters most.

When everything is pointed toward the purpose your team is unified around, there's a level of accountability that is much higher than anything a manager or boss could ever place on them. You've given your team freedom for social engagement, so they care about each other. Social pressure is much better than any pressure from a superior.

They have freedom, they get affirmation, they're part of a team that's pursuing this unified purpose, so each employee has an aspirational identity tied into working for your company. They become a better person because of this job. Their motivation for employment goes from "making money" or "providing for my family" to social impact. They want to make the world a better place, so they are willing to sacrifice and give of themselves to help others.

Through your unified purpose, their employment provides self-transcendence. That means that the employment you are providing quite literally makes them a better person.

But we can take this even a step further. Think about the person *you* are becoming by providing this for your employees. You aren't simply providing an income; you're providing a purpose to be achieved, together. You're providing a way for your team to become better people.

And as a result of this process, you yourself become a better person transcending to a new level of community leadership.

REBUTTAL

The biggest rebuttal you're most likely to have is that pointing everything toward your unified purpose feels overwhelming—and that is reasonable. Doing this correctly takes consistent, intentional actions.

However, you don't have to do everything all at once. Just take it one piece at a time and find the lowest-hanging fruit. Where can you implement the unified purpose first and easiest for you?

The first step I took when I implemented my unified purpose was changing the way our goals are set. Instead of tracking goals by number of transactions and dollars sold, we look at the number of people impacted by what we do.

Remember, too, that you can make adjustments to your unified purpose. You don't have to get it right on the first round. It doesn't have to be perfect by the time you're done reading this book. It took me years to get where I am today, and that's okay. In fact, even as I'm writing this book, I'm adjusting how we live our purpose in our accountability piece, with our living, breathing scoreboard.

Things take time. But as you work through it, you make it better every day, every week, every month, and every year. That's how you get to a point where your unified purpose is woven into every single piece of what you're doing, and it just changes everything.

LIVE WITH PURPOSE

My unified purpose is to genuinely love people through finances—even to the point where I say no to extra profit if it goes against that purpose.

The personal finance world is fraught with opportunities to put someone in a situation that may not be the best possible solution for them just so the company can get paid more, but I've structured my companies to intentionally love people through finances.

I started Stewardship Mortgage as a mortgage brokerage instead of a retail banking operation or correspondent lender because there is no argument that a broker is the absolute best solution for a consumer. Getting a loan through an independent mortgage broker gives you the best opportunity to have the lowest payments, the lowest out-of-pocket costs, and the lowest interest rates.

During the recession, a lot of people blamed the housing crisis on mortgage brokers, and as a result, a bunch of laws were passed that restricted the ways mortgage brokers were able to do business.

From the day I started my business, through the recession, right up until today, not one of my clients whom I helped get a mortgage ended up foreclosing on their loans. That never happened because I put their needs first and made sure they were able to afford their payments.

But I still had to change how I did business, under the law. It became more expensive and less profitable. A lot of mortgage brokers became corresponding lenders or retail bankers because they couldn't make money otherwise. But I knew that wasn't what was best for the customer.

I had to get smarter. I had to get more efficient and work harder. And as a result of those efforts, my total profit has increased every year since I've been in business—even through the hard times.

The same is true in the investment world and in financial planning. Other companies sell products that are masked to look like investments because they pay gigantic commissions—but they're terrible for the customer.

Putting a customer into an investment that is not in line with their financial goals means that person will have to work longer, they can't retire when they want, and they won't be able to spend as much time with their grandkids. I couldn't live with that selfishness.

I set up Stewardship to be a registered investment advisor, which means we do not get paid commissions based on the investment that we sell. We only get paid a percentage of the assets we manage. So if your assets go down, our amount goes down, too. When your assets go up, the amount we get paid goes up as well.

We make sure that how we're paid is in line with how well your investment is doing, because that is how we love people through finances.

Just the other day, somebody came to one of our team

members and said, "I want to buy an investment property to make some extra income." Most people would say, "Great! We'll go ahead and do this, and I'll get a big commission."

But my team is loving people through finances, so he looked at her situation genuinely and selflessly. He came to the rest of the team and said, "Guys, this person wants to do this investment. They qualify, and it would be a slam dunk, but I don't think it's the best investment for them because they have other areas of their finances that they should probably work on first. They have student loans, and I don't see that they're putting any money toward retirement. So if they add this passive income, that's going to impact their tax situation and increase their financial-risk profile."

The financial planners and investment advisors in our office scheduled an appointment to sit down and help our customer decide what she should do before investing in that property, even though she was all jazzed up about flipping a house after watching *Property Brothers*.

My employee lost several thousand dollars of commission that day by not originating the loan, but he went home happy because he knew that he made a positive impact on somebody's life—and he knows that when she is in the position to responsibly buy that property, she'll think of Stewardship first.

GIVE FREELY

You'll never have more enjoyment, joy, and satisfaction in your life as a business owner than when you're able to provide your team with a purpose and see them align with it. When you are living out that purpose yourself, you genuinely serve your team, your clients, and your community. You put their needs above your own, and that brings a crazy amount of satisfaction into your life.

When your team grabs ahold of this unified purpose and starts pursuing it with everything they've got, it'll bring tears to your eyes. They'd run through a brick wall for you. They'll do things that you never thought anybody would do for you. They respond by serving you because they're a part of your unified purpose. Unbelievable amounts of high-end performance, service, and love will come toward you—over and over and over again.

The heights of success that you can reach when your team is aligned with your unified purpose are immeasurable. You can't even imagine how amazing things will be.

KEY TAKEAWAYS

- Unifying people around a purpose starts with you, the leader. You then get buy-in from your team to be able to best serve your community. You can give meaning to how you lead and everything you and your team does by pointing it all to your unified purpose.

- If your purpose is "we should get rich," that is selfish and doesn't unify people. With a selfless purpose, however, your team can live out your mission every day.

- A unified purpose solves a problem and makes the world a better place. Every task you and your team do should be guided by your unified purpose.

MY INTENTIONAL ACTIONS

....

....

....

....

....

....

....

....

....

....

....

....

CONCLUSION

There is this culture among entrepreneurs and business owners to just grind, grind, grind and work, work, work. People want to be in the 5 a.m. Club and wake up before the sun rises. They wear this overworking mentality as a badge of honor, and if you're not doing those things, then the "hard-core" entrepreneurs look down on you.

I believe that the rise-and-grind-all-day-every-day culture is killing our society. It's damaging families. It's hurting relationships. We already spend way too much time away from the relationships we care about. This crazy work mentality leaves your spouse, your kids, your friends, and your family by the wayside. There are seasons where you have to put in a lot of work, but I don't believe it should be the norm. That belief is frustrating to me because it's self-serving and unsustainable, and I want to put an end to it.

I believe that having a team of people not only helps put an end to that culture, but it also helps you get to a healthy state. As you started reading this book, you may have felt frustrated with your work, feeling like it requires too much of you. You may feel trapped in your business. But that's not what work and businesses were created for.

Work was created to serve our communities. You can't serve your community well if you're not in a healthy place. If you're not sleeping, eating, and taking a break when you need one, you're going to hurt yourself. If your relationships aren't healthy, you're going to hurt yourself. And when you're not at your best, you won't be able to make the best kind of impact.

And you know what? I have a philosophical problem with that.

It is *just not right* that you feel like you have to wake up super-early every day because you are guilted into it by people with the rise-and-grind mentality. You might have a completely different circadian rhythm where you like to sleep in but you do great work later at night.

It is *just not right* to say that you shouldn't sleep a normal amount because you have to go, go, go. Sleeping four or five hours a day is going to make you sick—and steal years from your life. Studies show that if you don't sleep a minimum of six hours a day, you have a statistically higher chance of getting cancer.[28]

It is *just plain wrong* that business owners have to deal with nine out of every ten employees not giving their best. That is not okay. You deserve better—and so do they.

It is also *just plain wrong* that nearly 90 percent of employees go to a job every day that seems meaningless. They sacrifice unbelievable amounts of time away from their families without making an impact. Without doing work that matters. That they go to work because they have to, not because they want to. Our society, your community, deserves better, too.

This is wrong. So how can we change it?

Some of this can change by addressing it. I want to address this in hopes that it motivates you and helps relieve any guilt you may feel about that culture.

I am in the 8 a.m. Club—no, seriously. On a typical morning, I wake up between seven thirty and eight thirty. Some of you may be surprised by that. Did your opinion of me just subtly change? You might call that lazy—yet I own a mortgage brokerage, insurance agency, investment

---

28 https://thecancerspecialist.com/2018/04/10/
     researchers-are-studying-the-link-between-sleep-and-cancer/

advisory, and a financial planning firm. Those companies have grown to be *Inc.*'s 5,000 fastest-growing companies in America. I write about fifty blog posts a year, host a podcast and a YouTube channel, and I've created an online course where people can learn how to have an awesome company culture. Oh, and you're reading this book, so I'm also a published author!

I don't wake up early. I don't make rise-and-grind the norm. I take a month off every March and a few weeks every September to spend with my family. Weekly, I observe a Sabbath day to rest with my family, I take my wife on regular dates, I take my kids out consistently, and I'm obviously still able to get a lot done.

Why?

Because I have a great team. Having a great team not only helps get you away from that culture, but it also creates more bandwidth for you, so you have breathing room in your life to be healthy and for your relationships to be healthy.

WORK IS WORSHIP

I don't want you to walk away believing that I think work is bad. I don't; I think work is great. I believe that we were created to work—that's why it feels so good to do it.

I don't know your beliefs, but I am Christian and I believe that prior to the fall of man when there was no sin in the world, Adam and Eve were working. A lot of other people believe that because of sin we are required to work, and work sucks because of sin, but that isn't true.

According to Genesis, one of the purposes of man's creation is to toil the earth, to cultivate. We work to watch over it and protect it. That was our job. Every day, that was what Adam and Eve did—they worked!

I believe that I was put on this earth to worship the Lord. That's the bottom line. There are countless different, beautiful ways for me to worship God, and one of my favorite ways is through work. The effort that I put forth, the purpose that I'm living to make the world a better place and to love people through finances, to serve people—to me, that's a great opportunity to worship the Lord.

When you serve people, you are challenged. You grow. And many times, you end up receiving even more benefit than the people you're serving. You may think you're making an impact on people—and you are—but as you're sacrificing for and serving them, it ends up having an even greater impact on you.

I served in youth ministry, and many times the parents

of these high schoolers came up to me with tears in their eyes and thanked me for serving their kids. As I look back on my past experiences walking kids through from freshmen to seniors and the next thing I know I'm the officiant in their wedding, all I can say is, "Thank you for allowing me to serve your family because my life is significantly better as a result of it."

EMPLOYERS SERVE THEIR TEAMS, TOO

I genuinely try to serve every single one of my employees.

Prior to hiring somebody, my wife and I prayerfully go through a process where we choose to love that person. I even say in that final interview, "This may sound weird to you, but my wife and I decided that we're going to love you and we're going to love your family. We believe that's a choice that we act on with intentional actions, and that's what you're going to get here. I'm choosing to love you the best that I can throughout your employment."

We're not a huge company; we're still considered a small business. We haven't been around for a hundred years like other companies. The majority of our growth has happened within the last five years. We started with a small team of three people—with me doing way too much as owner-operator of the business for the first six or seven years of Stewardship's existence.

During the three-year period from 2016 to 2019, we won awards and accolades: top 35 entrepreneurs under the age of 35; best of our town in insurance, 2017, 2018, and 2019; best of our town mortgage company, 2019; mortgage brokerage of the year for the entire state of Arizona, 2016; top 1 percent loan originator; top 100 originator in the country. We have even been recognized by *Inc.* as one of the 5,000 fastest-growing companies in America.

Now we're a national brand with the ability to serve people throughout the country with their investment management, with home loans and insurance to follow soon.

This growth is all happening—more than I ever thought possible, we're getting more accolades, more awards, our P & L is headed in a higher positive direction than ever before—and I've been spending *less* time at the office, not more.

I've been speaking at conferences and events. My family and I have been able to go on more vacations.

Each of my three kids gets to go on a special daddy trip each year around their birthdays. Last year, my son and I went to Chicago for back-to-back Cubs game and Notre Dame Fighting Irish football game. My daughter and I also went to Chicago to visit a food bank and go to some Broadway shows.

My wife and I take a trip every year for our anniversary, where we evaluate our marriage and ask ourselves: What can we do more of? What can we do less of? What do we need to add? And what do we need to take away?

I'm able to do all of those as a result of the team I have. None of this would have been possible if I hadn't hired those employees.

BECOMING THE 12.3-PERCENTERS

Remember the 12.3 percent of people who *are* working up to their full potential? Those are the employees who are giving their absolute best when they are at work—and they are the people I choose to surround myself with in my company.

One of the hardest things I ever did was learning to trust people, especially at work. And they may not do things exactly the way I would do them—they do it a little bit differently, according to who *they* are—but they meet our purpose, and they make it all possible.

This level of success comes from bringing in a team of 12-percenters, giving them these three motivators, and trusting them enough to let them thrive.

They may not have been 12-percenters when they started,

but I knew they could align with our unified purpose. I knew they were selfless. And I knew they could pursue that purpose as part of our team—so I knew they could become part of that 12 percent.

I was able to attract the top talent because I had a unified purpose. I gave them freedom and affirmation and continually pointed everything toward that purpose, and our team became 12-percenters.

With your mindset shifted toward motivating with freedom, affirmation, and a unified purpose you point everything toward, you are set up to have a company culture full of people in that 12.3 percent who fulfill or exceed their potential.

With the people on your team fulfilling their potential, you're going to profit more, your business is going to grow, and things are going to be better.

Your employees want to be good at their jobs. We all want to be masters of our craft; that's why affirmation is such a big deal. You are giving your team the opportunity to get really good at something. When they know they're really good at it, they feel affirmed. They feel special. You're literally giving people a better life. You're giving them happiness, confidence, and hope.

Now you, too, can live in a neighborhood, a community, a society where more people are working to their full potential—and that is how we change the world.

Ideally, with enough people like you giving other people purpose, having an impact on society, and making the world a better place, we can shift those numbers. Instead of 12.3 percent of people giving their best at work and doing meaningful work, that number will be flipped and grow to 87.7 percent—or even 100!

That may sound crazy to some people, but that is my goal. I want more people to learn and understand how they can do this, too.

And it starts with you.

OUR PURPOSE

The really important part of changing that culture is to shift the focus away from us, the entrepreneurs, and onto the difference we are making in society.

YOUR PURPOSE

We are giving people jobs, and that's one of the biggest blessings you can do for your community, for our society, and for our country. You are quite literally making the world a better place because you are providing people with the opportunity to earn an income. They take that income and spend money, which ultimately helps our economy. When our economy does well, businesses do well.

And you're giving people something even more important than money: a purpose. You give your team's work meaning. You give them something to live for, and you give them hope. When they wake up every day, they have hope that this world is actually getting better—and they're a part of that. You're giving them a direct connection to make an impact on people and making society better.

This is your purpose.

How hypocritical would I be if I wrote a book telling you that you need to give your team purpose and then didn't give you one? Your purpose—larger even than the unified purpose for your company—is to run your business, lead your team, and give people the opportunity to make a difference.

MY PURPOSE—AND YOURS, TOO

My purpose in writing this book is to solve a problem. I found a solution that works for me and my team, and I'm confident that it will work for you and your team, too.

There's nothing extraordinary about me. I'm just another person, like you. I simply learned from my experiences, pursued the truth of how our brains operate, created a simple motivational hierarchy, and applied intentional actions every day.

The external problem I hope to solve is that too many people are stuck working *in* their business rather than being able to work *on* them because only 12.3 percent of people, total, are living up to their full potential at work.

How does that feel internally? That number hurts people. It causes frustration for employers and employees. And it creates a lot of waste in our society—not just throwing away money, but wasted talent, wasted impact that can be made on a society, and wasted mental energy from both employers and employees. Managers are pouring so much effort into trying to get the most out of their team that when they get home, they're exhausted. They have nothing left to pour into their family. They don't have time to work on their growing their business to make an even bigger impact.

Employees are also exhausted just doing tasks. Externally, they may be bored, but internally it's even worse: they don't have meaning in their life. Spending the bulk of one's day doing nothing but meaningless things leads to depression, anxiety, and other issues in our society.

That wasted talent could be poured into other endeavors, making a big impact on our communities through our businesses.

The philosophical problem is that it's *just plain wrong* that employers aren't getting the most out of their employees. It's not okay that people out there don't give their best.

It's also a problem that we have millions of businesses that don't provide great places for people to work. It's *just plain wrong* that many employees have only crappy places to work. It's not okay that CEOs don't learn any of this in business school, that business books teach one very traditional style but don't include any of these aspects.

All of this is *just plain wrong.*

Employers deserve more. Employees also deserve more. This hierarchy is going to help people get what they deserve *and* allow us to make a bigger impact on our community.

Employment is a big deal. Your business does awesome things, so you deserve to have a workforce that kicks butt! Our communities are filled with amazing people, and they should have places to work that are set up to allow them to thrive.

My hope is that you will unify with me around this purpose.

I hope that you get charged up about making a change. I want you to take intentional action, to turn your business around. The more people who read and act on what's in this book, the better chance we have at turning those stats on their head and making an absolutely huge impact on our communities. Employers can provide better products and services when they have better people working for them. Then our communities will have better places to work, and people will be able to do things that matter.

One step at a time, we can change our businesses, our communities—and the world.

REACH OUT

When you put this book down or stop the audiobook or click out of the e-book, I want you to take a look at everything you do within your business.

How do you currently motivate your team? How do you set goals? How do you hire people? Are you pointing everything to your unified purpose? Are you affirming people throughout those things? Do you give people freedom?

Continue to evaluate and make adjustments. Once you do, ask yourself, "Is money still number one in my business?" Or can you confidently say, "No, it's not number two or three either." Because the problem with employees has nothing to do with their paychecks; it has everything to do with the freedom, affirmation, and purpose you provide.

If you want more information and continued help, I have a ton of free resources you can use to go deeper:

- Subscribe to the Culture Course Show on YouTube: https://www.youtube.com/channel/UCeQFalsxcMrFG7MboVVp2-w
- Or subscribe to the Culture Course podcast on iTunes: https://podcasts.apple.com/us/podcast/culture-course/id1464755627
- Subscribe to my blog at https://www.culturecourse.com/blog
- You can even follow me on Instagram: @grantbotma. I post regularly and do a story almost daily on a topic relating to finances, company culture, or leadership.

Motivating your team with freedom, affirmation, and a unified purpose is just one section of changing your company's culture. A lot of other things have to be done to ensure that the people you have on your team thrive and want to stay. These aspects require a lot more training and information than can be included in one book.

If you are interested in exploring further, please feel free to check out my online course at https://www.culturecourse.com to learn how to keep your team thriving and take things to the next level. This course includes step-by-step video walk-throughs, guided instruction, copy-and-paste resources, and many other things that you can take from my business and insert into yours.

Inside Culture Course, you'll learn:

- My proven, eight-step template for hiring profitable employees
- How to onboard new employees who will stay with your company
- Compensation strategies that will allow you to attract and retain top talent
- How to set and reach company goals employees can get excited about
- How to keep your team accountable so they're accomplishing the tasks you want—without being micromanaged
- How to conduct employer reviews to get feedback on improving your company from the most important people who know your business best (and how to make sure your employees know that you care)

- The right way to conduct company meetings so they have a meaningful impact
- How to turn the process of terminating employees into a positive experience for both the business and the person you're letting go
- How to navigate building a virtual team while keeping remote employees connected and thriving
- Leadership development that will keep your team moving in the same direction

MEET YOUR THRIVING TEAM

You can have a thriving team.

Not only is it okay to break the mold of how other business owners are currently motivating, but it's easy and simple to do. Once you do, you will have a thriving team of people who will help change your life.

No longer will you work *in* your business. Now you will have the freedom to pursue the endeavors that you want to pursue.

No longer will you feel trapped in your company, held captive by never-ending tasks. Now you can do the things you want to do on a day-to-day basis, working *on* your business.

No longer will your company entangle itself in your life

and steal your free time. You will take back control and have the freedom to pursue the endeavors you actually *want* to pursue.

You won't even have to go to work daily in your business—and you can still add the value to your company that you have always dreamed of. You can put yourself in the position of CEO and have a self-managed team who works together with you on the mission of making a bigger impact. Because of your thriving team, you will do the things you've always wished were possible—at home, at work, and for the rest of your life.

ACKNOWLEDGMENTS

I was only able to write this book because of my team.

I want to acknowledge the fact that I had a team of people at the very beginning who had grace for me as I first got started trying to figure this out. I now have a team of people who are incredible at what they do.

My amazing team is made up of some of the best human beings on the planet—not just as employees but also as spouses, parents, aunts, uncles, friends, and members of our community. They're willing to say no to being paid the best in order to pursue a purpose of loving other people. They do work that matters and they sacrifice all the time to make a huge impact—and part of that sacrifice is financial. I want to acknowledge that and thank them for it.

Our purpose statement isn't just some statement painted on the wall—they are living it, every single day. Not a lot of people can say, "I want to love people through finances," but my team does—and that's the whole reason why I could write this book. That's the only reason I won awards. I wouldn't win anything without them. None of it happens without my team—every single individual who has ever been a part of Stewardship. They're unbelievably special people.

My team pursues our purpose just as I am able to pursue the mission of loving employers and employees through a motivational framework.

This book now has the possibility of making a huge impact on other people. Because of who the members of my team are and what they've done, other people now potentially have the opportunity to have a better workplace that gives their lives meaning.

I want to give you all credit and acknowledge each of you for that.

To Andrea Stahley, Ashton Pleasants, Brandon Ream, Brian Adams, Brian Baker, Brian Ream, Brianne Mortensen, Christina Romney, Christine James, Daniel Christy, Denise Gutwein, Dixye Wilson, Donna Rivituso, Emily Chavez, Greg Suiter, Jake Norton, Janell Bender,

Jarred Kuiper, Jean Klinkhamer, Jeremy Sharp, Jessica Tague, Jordan Stratman, Joseph Klein, Joy Stratman, Marshall Tague, Mike Zins, Ryan Delviken, and Samantha Marroquin: I love you and I'm proud of you.

ABOUT THE AUTHOR

GRANT BOTMA is the founder of Stewardship and was named a top entrepreneur before he reached the age of thirty-five. His team consists of nationally ranked producers who have won numerous awards, including Top 1%, Top 20 in the nation, Elite Producer, and more. Stewardship has been recognized as the "Broker of the Year" in Arizona, and Stewardship is an *Inc.* 5,000 Fastest-Growing Companies in America.

Not only are Grant's employees among the most productive in their field, but every single one of them loves their job. Grant's passion for behavioral science has led to unique success in creating a healthy company culture. His mission is to love people through knowledge, and he seeks to give his readers a better understanding of how to effectively lead and motivate a team of people.

Grant lives in Gilbert, Arizona, with his wife, Jodie, and three children, Cambria, Parker, and Ellenie. To learn more about Grant, please follow him on Instagram or Twitter @grantbotma, or you can connect with him on LinkedIn. For more details on creating a thriving culture for your company, you can check out his online course at https://www.culturecourse.com.

If you're interested in connecting with Grant personally, you can follow him on social media:

- Facebook: https://www.facebook.com/Culture-Course-277174859791250/
- Twitter: https://twitter.com/CultureCourse_
- LinkedIn: https://www.linkedin.com/company/cul-turecourse/
- Instagram: https://www.instagram.com/culture-course/

Made in the USA
Middletown, DE
26 February 2020

85350952R00120